HORSES GALORE HORSES GALORE
GALORE HORSES GALORE HORSES
HORSES GALORE HORSES GALORE
GALORE HORSES GALORE HORSES
HORSES GALORE HORSES GALORE
GALORE HORSES GALORE HORSES
HORSES GALORE HORSES GALORE
GALORE HORSES GALORE HORSES
HORSES GALORE HORSES GALORE
GALORE HORSES GALORE HORSES
HORSES GALORE HORSES GALORE
GALORE HORSES GALORE HORSES
HORSES GALORE HORSES GALORE
GALORE HORSES GALORE HORSES
HORSES GALORE HORSES GALORE
GALORE HORSES GALORE HORSES

Susan King

and

David Turnbull

Producer,
BBC TV's 'Horses Galore'
programme

HORSES GALORE

By arrangement with the
British Broadcasting Corporation
Pelham Books

Acknowledgements

Thanks are due to the following for their help and
advice : Tommy Hindley, Mrs Elizabeth Hayden,
Mrs P Turnbull, Bill Frith, Mr de Rivaz and
the British Horse Society.
    Finally, thanks must go to all the horsemen
and children whose generosity and love for horses
made the programme and this book possible.

PICTURE CREDITS

Photographs :
Tommy Hindley – 6, 9, 12, 13, 24, 25, 34, 35, 36, 37,
    41, 42, 43, 44, 45, 46, 47, 66, 67, 68,
    69, 74, 75, 76, 77, 78, 86, 87
BBC – 50, 51, 62, 63, 64, 65, 79
Kina Murray – 2 *bottom left, top right* and *bottom right,*
    3 *top left, top right* and *bottom right,*
    11, 59, 88, 90, 91
Clive Hiles – 20, 21, 29 *left*
Michael Roberts – 39, 40
Gordon Wood – 14, 15
W Pearson – 70
The Mansell Collection – 28, 38
David Jamieson – 10
Sorrel (courtesy Bill Frith) – 58
Elizabeth Hayden – 29 *right*
de Rivaz – 61
Photonews – 71, 72, 73
Leslie Lane – 54-55, 56-57, 80, 81, 82, 83
John Birt – 2 *top left,* 3 *bottom left* and *centre*
Lemah-Hamlen – 48

Line Drawings :
Norman Thelwell – 31 (©) 1978), 32-33 (©) 1979)
Jonathan Owen – 18-19
D Somerfield – 16, 17
Lesley Gowers – 22
John Birt – 27

Road safety diagrams on page 23 courtesy of the
    British Horse Society
Timetable and coach match notice on pages 52 and 53
    courtesy John Dick

First published in Great Britain by
PELHAM BOOKS LTD
52 Bedford Square
London WC1B 3EF
1979

ISBN 0 7207 1146 0

Designed by John Elsegood

Printed in Great Britain by
Ebenezer Baylis & Son Ltd, The Trinity Press
Worcester and London
and bound by Dorstel Press, Harlow

Contents

HOW IT ALL STARTED

I've been around horses all my life. Everyone in my family loves horses (everyone except my motorbike-mad brother Adrian) and we are particularly keen on the sport of driving. But how did I come to find myself on television with a show of my own? Well, it began one night when my father told me that the BBC were coming to make a film about how he trained ponies to drive in harness. By ten o'clock the next morning, the yard of our smallholding was full of cars. My father was surrounded and almost hidden by the film crew and their equipment – cameras, sound-recording machines, booms and tripods – and our ponies were hanging out of their boxes in amazement. I reckoned it was best to keep well out of the way. However, my father seemed to be enjoying it all and by lunchtime everyone was still in good humour.

During lunch I sat next to Sian, the producer's assistant, who told me about her job. It sounded far more attractive than any career I'd ever thought of doing, so that night I sat down to write to the BBC. Before I could post the letter though, the film crew were back, struggling into their wellies, ready for the second day's shooting.

The pony in the film story was to be taken out on the road for the first time. This part of the training is usually done with my father walking behind the pony, driving it with long reins, while I walk in front leading it. So to my surprise, I was going to have to be in the film after all.

That night when everyone had gone, the yard seemed very quiet and empty. I helped my father feed the ponies and posted my letter.

A few days later we would see the BBC crew again; this time they were to film us competing in a driving event at a show in Wokingham, Berkshire. For this sequence we would use 'Cusop Blighter' our famous Welsh Mountain Pony stallion. Cusop has won more rosettes, cups and championships than any other harness pony, but even so, things can still go wrong – and it had been decided that I should drive! However, Cusop really did his stuff and when the judge pinned on the winner's rosette and handed me a beautiful silver cup it was a perfect ending to the film and the story.

Unbeknown to me that little film was to be the start of another story, as I discovered when the producer phoned me. The BBC were looking for someone to present a whole series of 'Country Search' programmes. At first I thought the producer was pulling my leg, but he wasn't. After a long association with 'Country Search' I was offered the job of presenting 'Horses Galore', which gave me a wonderful opportunity to meet some of the people who breed, ride, drive and work with horses.

This book is a glimpse behind the scenes of the horse world, and a look back at some of the fascinating topics which were featured in the programmes.

And to think that it all began with a little pony called Cusop.

Left: Cusop Blighter, without whom none of this would have been possible.

★
MARY CHIPPERFIELD
★

If Mary Chipperfield hadn't decided to continue working in the circus, training her famous circus horses, she would probably be one of the best dressage riders in the world. Her love and command of animals is tremendous and one can only admire her.

Mary lives in a small village in Hampshire, and spends most of her time there, apart from when she is on tour. Also resident at her home are horses, llamas, camels – in fact almost everthing you would *not* imagine living in the English countryside !

Mary also has some Grevy's Zebras, a type of zebra that is considered to be untrainable, but Mary has won them over and they are now a very important part of her act. She has to give them plenty of exercise before they come on though, as they tend to be rather too exuberant.

The most important thing I learnt from Mary when I visited her, was that training horses for the circus requires a tremendous amount of time and patience. Without a doubt Mary sincerely loves the animals she works with, and it was a great privilege to watch her at work.

The type of horse best suited for circus work must be able to catch the public's eye. They must also be sound, hardy, and, above all, intelligent. Mary chooses Arabs. Not only do they have all the qualities mentioned, but also they are a convenient size, being fairly small, around 14 – 15 h.h. They are extremely intelligent animals and have the right temperament for the type of work they are expected to do. Apart from all this, they are a beautiful breed of horse. The Arab has a certain presence and elegance and is renowned for his small head and 'dished' face. Their pace is light and 'brilliant', covering the ground with great ease and grace. Most of the Arabs in Mary's act are stallions ; their manner is one that is proud, and they also seem to take to the task quicker.

Top: Mary believes that kindness and patience – plus the odd titbit – are the only way to train horses.

Centre: Teaching horses to rear requires many helpers.

Bottom: It can take weeks of patient work to achieve this result.

Left: Mary Chipperfield and her supposedly untrainable zebras.

Mary trains her horses on the principle of association of ideas ; as soon as a horse has understood a new trick or lesson he is rewarded and given a titbit, such as a horse-cube. When a new trick is being developed or taught, endless patience is necessary. The animals are never punished. It is up to the trainer to take the time to explain each new exercise before progressing to another.

Mary emphasises that you cannot hit a horse to make him do what you want ; if you do, he will be afraid of you. When a trainer has a whip in his or her hand, it is merely a lengthening of the arm. If you want a horse to go a little faster, because you are not near enough to touch him with your hand, you touch him with the whip. To slow him up, the whip

should be placed in front of him; and when the whip is held up high, he should learn to stop – all by association of ideas. But the horse must learn to respond to the whip before all else. In a circus ring, with the music playing and the crowd clapping and talking, the horse would never hear the trainer's voice – the whip is the only form of communication.

One of the first tricks a horse is taught is that of rearing. It's a trick which takes a lot of patience and a great amount of time. As with most tricks, a lot of work is done on the lunge rein, and this is no exception.

In the ring with her, Mary has four or five assistants, a necessity where this trick is concerned. First a lunge rein is clipped to either side of the horse's mouth and held by two assistants. To the horse's foot another lunge rein is attached, but only tied. Should the horse get into difficulty, the knot will easily come undone.

Mary stands in the middle of the ring with the whips, which by now the horse has come to understand. She gently touches the free front leg with one of the whips. As she does this, the helper holding the rein attached to the other front leg, gently pulls on the rein. Mary then raises her whip and gives the command.

Only by continual practice over a long period of time will the horse understand what is wanted of him. Each time he does it he will be rewarded until, in the end, he rears perfectly, and his trainer has something of which to be proud.

The King's Troop

The Musical Drive of the King's Troop has become one of the British army's most spectacular displays, and its history is one that is just as grand.

Before the Second World War, a succession of horse artillery batteries were stationed in London. The last of these was mechanised in 1939 and it was His Majesty King George VI's wish that after the War, a troop of Royal Horse Artillery, mounted and dressed in traditional manner, should once again take part in all ceremonies of state. It was also His Majesty's wish that the troop should be known as the 'King's Troop'.

Her Majesty Queen Elizabeth II has decided that the troop should continue to honour her father and keep the name that he gave them.

The ceremonies they take part in include the firing of all royal salutes in Hyde Park; these occur on royal anniversaries and state occasions. The troop also provides a gun carriage and a team of black horses for state and military funerals, and turns out on Armistice Day, the Lord Mayor's Show and The Queen's birthday.

The King's Troop regularly practise their famous drive on Wormwood Scrubs.

The King's Troop is a highly trained unit of about two hundred men, nine officers (one being a veterinary surgeon) and more than one hundred horses. The men are divided into six sub-sections and each group is responsible for a gun and all its necessary equipment.

The Musical Drive is carried out at the gallop and in very small arenas which measure only 90 yards by 30 yards. You may wonder just what is so marvellous about this – well, each team of horses pulls *two tons* of gun and limber behind them and there are *no* brakes! Needless to say, the horses and riders have to be extremely fit. Because the horses are pulling such a heavy weight at speed, great accuracy and keen judgement are absolutely vital to avoid accidents.

The atmosphere at these displays is electric and you really do get caught up in the excitement. The most thrilling part of the display is the famous scissors movement, when the teams criss-cross the centre of the arena with little to spare between the gun of the first team and the lead horses of the second team. It is absolutely terrifying to watch. Great confidence is needed by everyone – one slip could mean disaster!

The horses and soldiers all live at the barracks in St John's Wood, London, where virtually each man has a horse to look after. The horses are of no particular breed and most of them come from Ireland. Purchased when they are about four or five years old, they are the right age to be broken-in, first to the saddle and then to harness. But it's not just the horses who are trained but the

It takes four soldiers to pull the heavy gun.

men as well.

Young men wishing to join the Troop may be employed in many different trades. Recruiting is done through advertising in magazines such as *Horse and Hound*.

There are many different trades you can take up, such as farriery, saddlery, tailoring, storekeeping, vehicle driving and, of course, working with horses. But no matter what you join as or who you are, you will learn to ride. It helps if you have any riding experience as this will put you at a considerable advantage in your early training.

That basic training consists of some very hard exercises, as I discovered! Bending over and touching your toes may sound easy but I certainly found it difficult! Jumping is also taught and many soldiers are encouraged to take part in competition riding, such as show-jumping, horse trials and hunter trials.

It is certainly a very hard life and I think you have to be really dedicated. Up at six o'clock, horses groomed and ready to go out on the road for exercise by 6.30 prompt. After exercise the horses are returned to the barracks, rubbed down and fed.

The horses are fed four meals a day. This may sound a lot but working horses such as these need plenty of nourishment if they are to remain fit and healthy. Each is fed according to his work, his type, condition, temperament and size. And though the horses have official names and numbers, the soldiers know them by their stable names.

It's interesting to note that the original three-day event was known as the Military and, in fact, was designed to test the skill and training of officers and their mounts in all disciplines, i.e. dressage, cross-country and show-jumping. The horses had to have immense stamina and courage, as in the three-day event of today.

My thanks to Major Mike Webster and Sergeant-Major John Emmerson for showing me the marvellous drive of The King's Troop. It was terrific! If you get the chance to see the Musical Drive, be prepared to hang on to your seat belts!

Above: Inside one of the stables.

Right: Saddlery is just one of the many trades you can take up while serving with the Troop.

Below: New recruits are given basic riding instruction – it's hard work too, as I discovered.

Appleby Fair is the best-known Gypsy horse fair in the country. It was started in 1750 for the trade of horses, sheep and cattle, but over the years the Gypsies made it their own and turned it into a horse fair. Gypsy people have always had a special knowledge and love of three things, namely music, metal and horses, and they still make their living out of them. The horse and the Gypsy have been inseparable for hundreds of years ; the life of the Gypsy family depended on it and revolved around it. A family without horses was finished.

But who are the Gypsies ? Very little is known about them and what they know they keep to themselves. To the rest of us they remain a most puzzling and mysterious people. Wherever you travel in Europe you will find Gypsies, keeping to their own way of life, laws and language.

All Gypsies of all nationalities have a common language – Romany. It's very, very old and was handed down from father to son, never written, because most Gypsy people didn't read or write. For many years now experts have believed that this language, Romany, holds the clue as to where the Gypsies came from. It seems to be Indian in origin, but no one knows when or why the Gypsies left India to start their wanderings.

They appeared in Persia about the year 850 AD and by 1417 they arrived in Europe. They made such a nuisance of themselves in England that in 1530 Henry VIII gave them sixteen days to get out of the country. The Gypsies paid no attention and by Elizabeth I's time there were over ten thousand of them, and they had become a part of English life.

In the early days they travelled with pack donkeys and horses and lived in rod tents, made from ash poles and very thick felt

Washing the horses in the River Eden at Appleby.

14

blankets pinned together with long thorns from a blackthorn bush. Then, in the 1850s a new sight and sound came to the roads of England – the Gypsy caravan. This home on wheels was the Gypsy's most famous and valuable possession.

As with everything to do with Gypsies, no one really knows when and how these caravans first came into being, although they were probably in use on the Continent long before they arrived here. It is likely that they evolved bit by bit from the carts the Gypsies were already using.

These early waggons were all individually made as, at that time, the English Gypsy was very prosperous, much better off than the Gypsies on the Continent. The most famous type of waggon was the Bow Top. It was much lighter than the others, so a family could travel much further in a day, maybe as much as twenty miles. They'd start early in the morning and rest during the heat of the day while the men would look for work or a 'deal' and the horses would graze at the road side.

Looking after the horses was

the first job to attend to when a caravan had pulled on to a 'pitch' for the night. There was usually good grazing on the roadsides but sometimes the Gypsy would slip the horses into a farmer's field at night and take them out before the farmer was up in the morning.

The coming of the lorry and the motorway saw the end of the horse-drawn waggon, but today, at fairs like Brough and Appleby, the 'travelling nation' still comes together each year to buy, sell and 'deal' in horses.

The site of the fair at Appleby is on what is now called Fair Hill, high in the Cumberland hills. The fair is held in early June, when the hill becomes a glittering sea of waggons, trailers and brand-new cars.

So great is the attendance that families spill out into all the nearby lanes in an attempt to find somewhere to 'pull'. Horses are tethered all along the verges and the crowd is so thick that it is almost impossible to move. The old horse-drawn waggons, or 'vardos', have pride of place on the hill and nowhere is the Gypsy passion for bright colour and design better seen.

Down in the old grey-stone town of Appleby, the streets throng with men and horses, and children are seen taking horses to the river to wash them. A country lane, once a Roman road,

A narrow Roman road serves as a market place.

serves as a market place. Here the men and boys run the horses up and down to show them off, just as they would have done hundreds of years ago. Buyers gather round and bargaining begins. Each time a buyer makes a bid he slaps the palm of the seller's hand. Cash, often a large sum, is paid on the spot, and some horses will change hands several times during the fair.

In the early evening, trotting races are held on a grass track by a stream, where a natural bank gives everyone a perfect view. The race is a mile long, and the horses are graded and run in heats so that they are evenly matched.

Bow-top waggon
showing interior, rear & offside

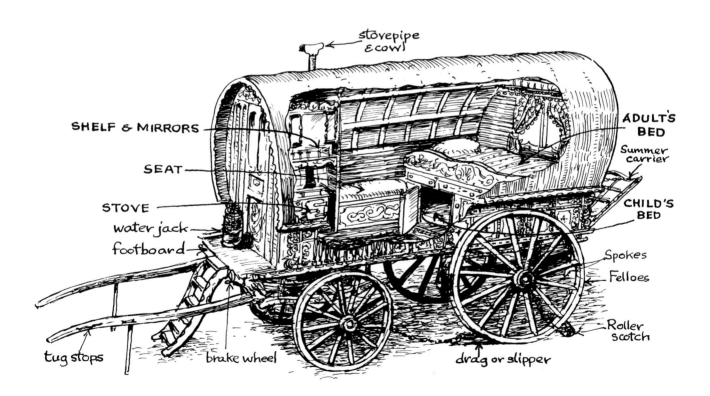

stovepipe & cowl

SHELF & MIRRORS

SEAT

STOVE

water jack

footboard

ADULT'S BED

Summer carrier

CHILD'S BED

Spokes

Felloes

Roller scotch

tug stops

brake wheel

drag or slipper

Bow-top

Reading

Four well-known types of Gypsy waggon.

Ledge

Burton

The Horse of the Year Show

The Horse of the Year Show is held in October every year at Wembley and lasts for a whole week. It was begun by Col. Sir Michael Ansell and first came to Wembley in 1958. Since then it has become the Wimbledon of show-jumping, attracting great champions and brilliant newcomers from all over the world. But it is more than this, being the last great show of the season, many national competitions come to a climax there.

Starting at 8.30 am and going on until 11 pm there are dressage events, driving and riding club

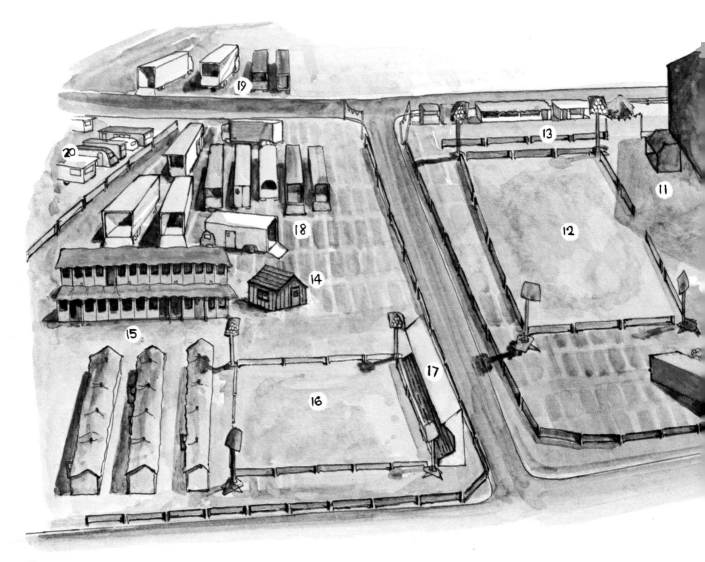

championships, showing and in-hand competitions, the Pony Club mounted games and championships for police horses and junior show-jumpers.

Over a thousand horses take part, bringing with them riders, drivers, grooms and owners. Half will spend the week there, the horses in temporary stables, the competitors in a little 'town' of caravans next to the horse lines – and all in a car park in the middle of north London.

Each day the show is run like clockwork by 'control' at the side of the arena, where Show Director John Stevens is in touch with collecting-ring stewards, the course builder and his arena party, judges and timekeepers. Here too sit the commentators, linked to the BBC outside broadcast vans. Millions of people watched on television last year and 65,000 more came to enjoy this wonderful show.

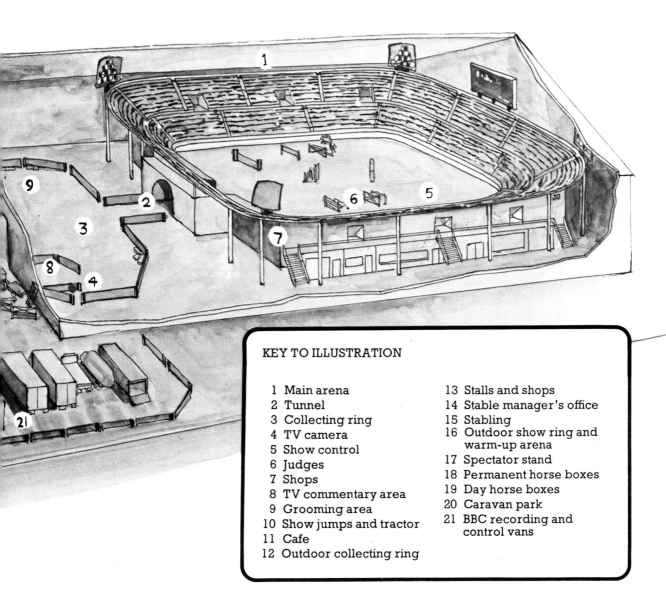

KEY TO ILLUSTRATION

1 Main arena
2 Tunnel
3 Collecting ring
4 TV camera
5 Show control
6 Judges
7 Shops
8 TV commentary area
9 Grooming area
10 Show jumps and tractor
11 Cafe
12 Outdoor collecting ring
13 Stalls and shops
14 Stable manager's office
15 Stabling
16 Outdoor show ring and warm-up arena
17 Spectator stand
18 Permanent horse boxes
19 Day horse boxes
20 Caravan park
21 BBC recording and control vans

The Horse of the Year Show is packed with exciting and memorable moments. For some the highlight of the show is the Musical Drive of the Heavy Horses, for others it is the Parade of Horse Personalities of the Year or perhaps the final round of the Pony Club Mounted Games Championship for the Prince Philip Cup. Here are a few of the people I met and some of the moments that I specially enjoyed.

THE BANWEN BRANCH OF THE PONY CLUB

Of the three hundred Pony Club teams which enter the competition only six win through to Wembley. The games are run off over five days, the teams competing every afternoon and evening, and spending a whole week amongst the top riders and horses.

The Banwen is a tiny branch from south Wales with only thirty-five members. Their practice ground is on top of an old coal tip, and their trainer works underground all week. Two of the ponies work daily shepherding on the hills and most of the children have to hack a good five miles to practise, whatever the weather and often in the dark. Now the ponies had to get used to the bright lights and the roar of the crowd. On the first night they came last, but in the most exciting final ever seen they went on to win the Cup for Wales for the first time in twenty years.

ALAN BALL

Jumping indoors is different from jumping outside – the space is very limited, yet the horse has to be allowed as much room and flow to the fences as possible. Alan Ball has been designing and building the courses at Wembley for sixteen years : 'I plan the complete course layout, the types of fences, the heights, colours and distances. My course builders get a copy about a month before the show. They colour it in to make it easier to understand. If it's a blue fence, they put a blue line ; if it's a red parallel they put two red lines ; if it's a green staircase they put three green lines. They put the heights on in pencil because during the day I might decide I've been a bit strong or not strong enough. You want five or six clear rounds to make a good competition, so you have to look at the riders and the horses all the time. And of course you've got to make it exciting yet end on time.'

CATHRYN COOPER

Thirteen-year-old Cathryn Cooper from Northumberland and her famous pony Holly of Spring made history at the show by winning the title 'Show Pony of the Year' for the fourth time.

Unbeaten in their first season in 1975 and winners of the Championship ever since, Cathryn agreed it was hard work, but fun : 'I always put Vaseline on her muzzle and around her eyes to make her shine, and wear a button hole to match my tie and hair ribbons. It's very important that you've got the correct clothes and your hair is right and everything's clean and smart. It's called the *show* ring and if the horse is going to look good, so must you.

'Holly has a natural presence

A lap of honour for the victorious Banwen.

Cathryn and Holly. (I wonder if Cathryn is singing?)

and beautiful action. But when she's in front of the judges she usually droops her ears, so I started singing to her, to keep her ears pricked and it worked.'

Now that she is seven Holly has retired to stud and Cathryn wants to turn to eventing and hunter trials.

THE MUSICAL DRIVE OF THE HEAVY HORSES

Six teams of horses take part, each driven by a horseman on foot, and to see these horses waiting in the collecting ring, all plaited up in their red plumes and patent-leather show harness, is an unforgettable sight.

Preparing these magnificent horses and presenting them at their best is an art. By skilfully placing the plaits and ribbons Harry Ransom, the head

horseman at Young's Brewery, can improve the shape of a horse's neck or show off its powerful quarters.

'I find that strapping and cleaning a horse with a dandy brush is a lot better than washing. I think people have a tendency to wash nature out of the body. I wash only the mane, tail and legs, and dust the white bits with a little baby powder before we go in.'

Next year Harry plans to drive the biggest pair of Shires in the country: Henry Cooper 18.2 h.h. and Samson 18.1 h.h. That should be something to see.

THE HERMES CONCOURS d'ELEGANCE

A new competition at the show is the final of the Hermes Concours d'Elegance. Competitors are judged on their costume, turn-out and overall impression. Throughout the year driving turn-outs all over the country try to qualify for a place at the Horse of the Year Show.

The twelve who were chosen provided some wonderfully elegant and colourful turn-outs. I specially liked a lady in purple with a huge white feather in her hat, and a mother and child all in black and white, and there was a carriage with big yellow wheels with a dalmation (the original carriage dog) trotting elegantly behind.

The winner was the youngest driver of all, a little girl from Wales, called Alison. She wore a plum-coloured costume and drove a grey pony to a plum-coloured dog-cart.
She was only eleven and beaming with delight because

apart from anything else she had just beaten her mother!

THE POLICE HORSE OF THE YEAR

In this competition the horses are judged firstly for conformation and quality – they must be big and have good strong legs and feet for all the road work they have to do.

The turn-out has to be immaculate and, of course, there are several very interesting extra pieces of tack, such as the chain worn round the horse's neck, in case someone cuts the reins.

Finally, the best compete in the main arena, in a stiff test of horsemanship and obedience. The horse and officer have to negotiate a series of hazards such as they might meet in extreme conditions in the street.

They had to ride boldly through a high wall of cardboard boxes which tumbled down around them; walk carefully over a row of dummies, representing people, without stepping on them; walk across planks and through an archway of fluttering plastic strips. Finally they had to negotiate their way through a cheering, jeering crowd who were beating drums, blowing trumpets and waving banners, the test ending with a startling revolver shot.

Throughout it all the horse had to go forward obediently and boldly.

It was a most impressive performance and a great tribute to the incredible standard of horsemanship achieved. Long may they be seen on the streets of Britain.

Road Safety

Sooner or later everyone who rides is going to have to cope with a horse in traffic, and even the most experienced riders can suddenly find themselves in danger. Sadly, any accident involving a horse is likely to be serious.

Though many accidents are caused by drivers who simply don't realise that a horse can be taken by surprise, frightened and get out of control, do riders themselves always give road safety enough thought? It's not always the motorist's fault.

Remember, every day, somewhere in this country, a horse is killed on the road, no doubt bringing suffering and injury to the people involved. So it's important for riders, especially young riders, to do everything they can to lessen the risk.

The British Horse Society have devised a riding and road safety test which is free and open to everyone. They have also published a small manual which everyone should read called *Ride Safely*. In 1978 it cost 30p, which doesn't seem much when you consider how costly an accident can be.

The most important thing to remember is that you are not the only person using the road. You should always make sure that other people know what you intend to do. When making a signal, make it and mean it.

Training your horse to be reliable in traffic is vital. A young horse can place you in great danger if he plays up, and the road is no place to school him

Familiarise him in stages. Never risk an accident. Introduce him to the sight and sound of traffic from the safety of a field; progress to letting him get used to a car in a quiet lane or drive. Lead him then ride him past, then let the car pass him. Reward him all the time and make a fuss when he does well.

Now he can be introduced to traffic on a road. Find a wide grass verge on a quiet road, put on a

I intend to move out or turn to my right.

Please STOP. Don't be afraid to stop motorists if you think they are putting you at risk.

I intend to pull in or turn to my left.

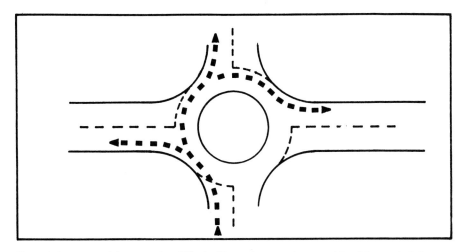

Negotiating a roundabout can be difficult. Always keep to the near side of the road all the way round the roundabout until you come to your exit, otherwise you will have traffic on both sides of the horse. Watch for traffic on the right and give clear signals of your intentions.

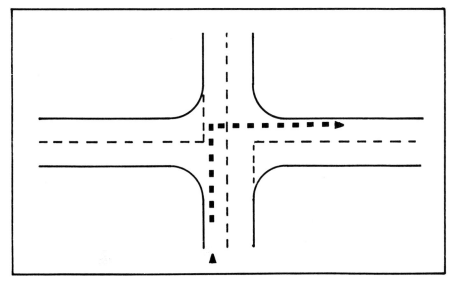

When turning right at cross roads and T-junctions, keep to the near side up to and beyond the centre of the junction to prevent traffic getting on the inside of the horse, then signal clearly and when safe turn into the near side of the intended route.

strong headcollar and long lead rope. Take a feed bowl, and a steady reliable horse to keep him company. Be patient, remain calm and he will settle.

Before you ride him on the road, get him used to as many hazards as you can think of, in a yard or field, motorbikes starting up, radios being turned on suddenly, things that flap and flutter, brightly painted cones, dogs, doors banging. Use your imagination and make much of him. Give him confidence.

When you first go out on the road, choose a quiet moment, and make sure he's not fresh. Try and get an experienced horse to accompany him and act as a shield from the traffic. As the young horse becomes confident the two can swap places and then, in turn, he can go out alone.

Don't ride with your pony's head turned in towards the side of the road. Let him see the traffic and keep his head turned out. If he gets a fright he will then swing away from the traffic into the side of the road.

Remember, wet roads are noisy and your horse may get very frightened if he gets splashed.

Never take risks, look and think ahead at all times. One day your life may depend on it.

Plaiting a Mane

The first thing to do when plaiting your horse or pony's mane is to decide which method you are going to use. For instance, at home we entwine wool in the plait, but you can use elastic bands or even sew the plait.

We use blue wool, to match the colour of the gig which we use in the driving classes. Always, the day before the show, Cusop is washed unless, of course, it's too

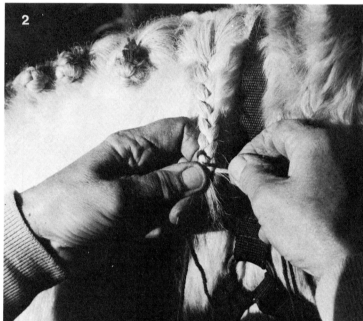

1. Divide the section to be plaited into three strands and start plaiting in the usual way.

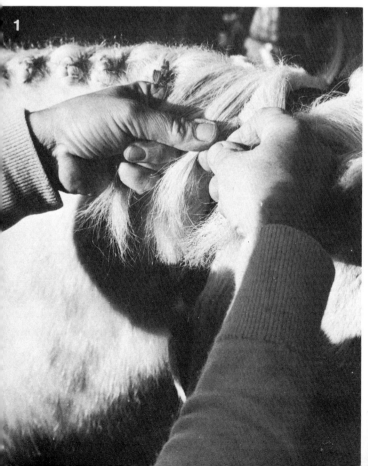

2. About threequarters of the way down start to plait your wool into the mane.

3. After tying off tightly at the bottom of the plait, twist the whole plait into a small, neat knot.

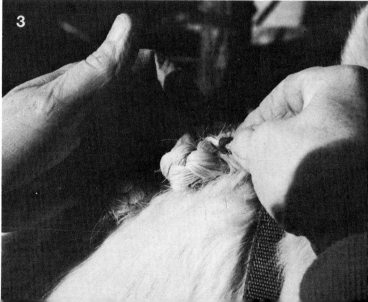

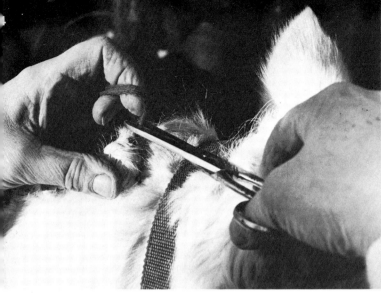

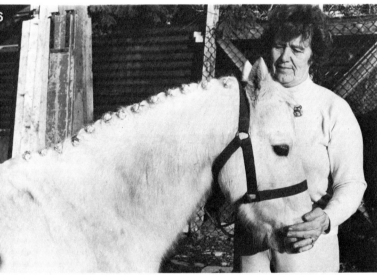

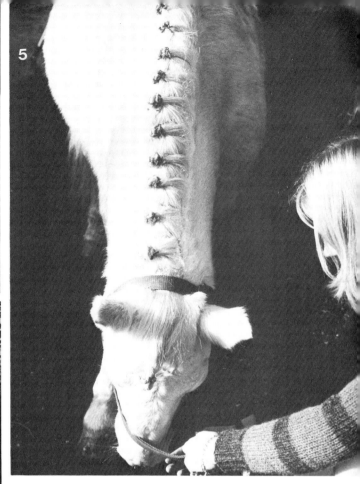

4. Wind the wool around the base of the knot, tie off, then trim away surplus wool.

5. The fully plaited mane, as seen from above . . .

6. . . . and from the side.

cold. We never wash his mane on the day of the show as this makes his hair too fine to handle.

You will normally be able to make at least nine plaits on a horse's mane but with Cusop we often find that we get as many as thirteen.

To start, divide the mane into nine (or more) equal parts, (this you can do visually but some prefer to measure it out allowing, say, a comb's width for each section). Each section of mane is then divided into three and plaited in the normal way, firmly and neatly, starting at the forelock and working down the mane.

About threequarters of the way down each plait, take a piece of wool twine, which should be about 8-9 inches long and can consist of three thicknesses of wool, and start to plait it into the mane (as shown in the illustration).

Tie the wool at the bottom of the plait to prevent the plait from coming undone. Then twist the whole plait into a knot as tightly and as neatly as you can. Tie the remaining ends of the wool around the bottom of the knot so that it is good and firm.

Finally, cut off the ends of the wool and you should have a perfect plaited mane.

We, or should I say my mum, usually manage to plait a whole mane in about threequarters of an hour. It is something which needs practice!

Building Your Ow

Show-jumping is an exciting and fun sport which is now very popular both here and abroad. Actually I know very little about it, though I did once have a go at Olympia (and you can see what Norman Thelwell thought of my efforts on p. 30).

(and you can see what Norman Thelwell thought of my efforts on p. 30).

Sally Ennor is a young show-jumper who lives near me and was in the British Junior Show-jumping Team when they competed in Belgium in 1977. I made the following notes after talking to her.

First of all you've got to make or buy your jumps. Buying them is expensive, so try to persuade your father to help you make them. The poles should be 12 foot long, heavy and strong. Thin, light poles are hard for the pony to see and flimsy fences make for carelessness. The wood for the wings needs to be heavy and strong and bolts should be used for any joints. The wings should be able to withstand a few knocks and nails would obviously be very dangerous.

Tyres and oil drums are popular but use them with care as horses can catch their legs in tyres and on upright oil drums, resulting in a nasty fall. If you want to use oil drums, lay them down and put blocks on either side to prevent them rolling about when you're jumping.

You will need about seven fences – that's a good average course of the sort you'll meet in novice classes. Try and include one double or a combination of three. Try to get as much variety as possible in your fences and lots of different colours. In time you'll be able to make or find lots of different 'fillers' for your jumps; e.g. brush wood, wall units, palisades and planks.

When laying out your course or track, give it two changes of rein (or direction), but don't make it too tricky or testing. It should be inviting and fun for your pony. Our drawing shows the layout.

The first fence is a **rustic fence** and should encourage the pony to start jumping. Never build the first fence going away from the gate. It's always much easier to jump towards 'home' over a simple, easy fence.

The second fence is an **upright,** again not too difficult, to encourage the horse to keep going.

Next comes a **parallel** with planks, to make your horse spread out a little bit more and open out over the fence.

This is followed by a turn and another **upright** with a palisade or a board underneath, so that the fence isn't too 'gappy'. The ground line is very important. You want your pony to look down and see what it's jumping. If you have a good ground line it will pick up and jump well, so if necessary put a spare pole on the ground in front of any fence which hasn't got a good ground line.

The fifth fence is a **triple bar,** ascending like a staircase, to really open your horse out. But make sure you ride to the front pole – if you ride to the back pole you'll stand off too far and land on the back pole.

The sixth fence, the **stile,** is to test your pony's obedience. It is a narrow fence with a brush filler underneath. Disobedient ponies will run out instead of going through the middle.

The seventh and last fence is a **double,** a palisade with a parallel bar, then one stride to an upright with a wall underneath. Try to keep the double all one colour. Don't have a blue and white going in and a pink and yellow coming out or you may startle your pony unnecessarily.

You can work out the strides between fences in a combination or double fence on the basis of 24 feet to one pony stride and $34\frac{1}{2}$ feet to two pony strides.

Don't jump your pony every day or he will get stale and won't jump well for you.

After you've jumped three times the same way, change the course or move the jumps to avoid making holes in front of the jumps and on the landing side. Unlevel ground will unbalance your pony and jumping in and out of holes will damage his legs.

Try and build your course on the best and most level ground you can find. No ground is too good if you want your pony to enjoy jumping and jump well without fear of stumbling or becoming unbalanced.

Jumping Course

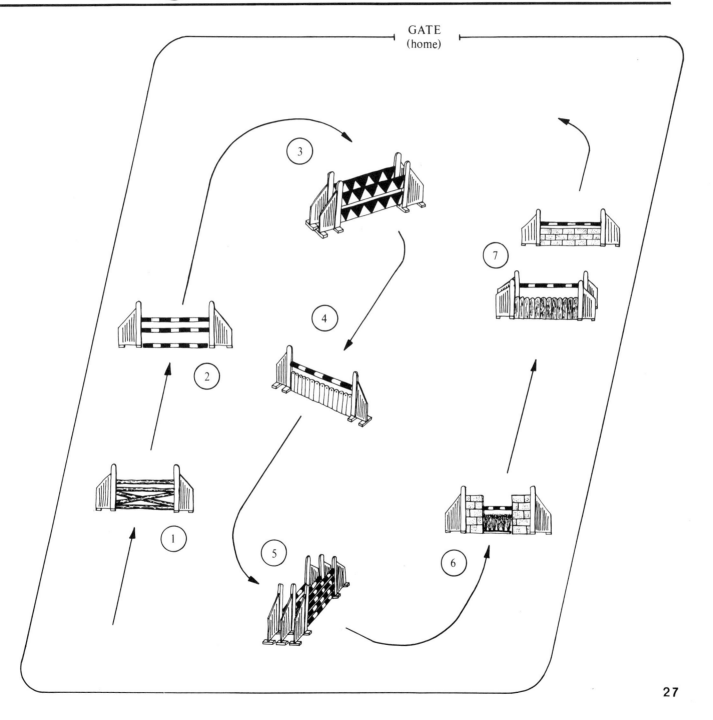

GATE
(home)

27

THE CASPIAN HORSE ~ LOST FOR 3000 YEARS

The origins of the Caspian Horse are lost in time but, even so, this tiny horse has a long and fascinating history. The native wild horse of Iran, it was last heard of in the seventh century AD. Then, for over a thousand years, the Caspian was believed to be extinct until one day, in the spring of 1965, it trotted back into the record books.

A tiny bay stallion, darting about the streets of a bazaar in Amol, northern Iran, caught the eye of Mrs Louise Firouz. The little animal was about the size of a donkey and just as overworked, but it dashed around the narrow alleyways with its cart at great speed.

Its fine head, large eyes, slender bones and gaily carried tail set it apart from the other horses plodding along with their loads.

Out of sheer curiosity Mrs Firouz bought the 'pony' and had it taken in a truck to Norouzabad, just outside Tehran. Gradually a few more tiny horses like the little stallion were found in the rice fields near the shores of the Caspian Sea. Hence the name, Caspians.

Most were covered in sores, ticks and lice, but they were enthusiastically welcomed by the pony-starved children at Norouzabad.

The miniature horses soon showed themselves more than capable of everything they were asked to do : pony racing, where their speed was invaluable ; gymkhanas ; driving in harness, where their strength and lovely floating action came into their own ; and when stud stallions were ridden by children everyone realised the Caspian's incredible temperament. It was not long, of course, before the children tried show-jumping and the 'ponies' were 'popping over' three-foot fences.

So successful were their exploits that more Caspians were found and brought to Tehran to form the nucleus of a breeding herd. Their number grew to twenty-three, which became difficult to maintain privately. The Crown Prince of Iran bought the Caspians and the Royal Horse Society of Iran took over their management.

The Royal Horse Society of Iran is dedicated to the preservation and improvement of Iran's native breeds. But what was this miniature horse ? It was pony-sized, yet looked like a horse. And where had it come from ? All sorts of experts were approached ; archaeologists zoologists, specialists in horse breeding ; laboratory studies of blood, bone and skin were taken. Slowly the evidence was pieced together. Detailed analysis showed that in spite of its tiny size it was indeed a horse.

Could this be, then, the ancient horse of the Persians ? For years archaeologists had noticed these tiny horses in carvings and had thought that the small size of the horses was due to lack of space.

The difficult task of tracing the descent of the Caspian began. At first the only proof of their

Left: The trilingual seal of Darius the Great (*c.* 500 BC) showing a pair of tiny horses pulling the royal chariot in a lion hunt.

existence was found at the Palace of Persepolis where they appear in the same carving with bigger horses. The trilingual seal of Darius the Great, now in the British Museum, shows a pair of tiny horses with very slim legs, small ears and slightly convex faces, pulling the royal chariot on a lion hunt (*c*.500BC). Later, remains of miniature horses were found mixed up with the bones of 16-17 h.h. horses from 650 BC on.

Much of the excitement in tracing the Caspian's history lay in the fact that it might turn out to be the ancestor of the Arab horse, one of the four principal breeds (Exmoor, Fell and Ardennes are the other three) from which all domestic horses descend.

Suddenly, the whole history of the legendary Caspian emerged, startlingly clear and stretching back to 3000 BC. This tiny horse was the most ancient domestic breed in existence.

Mrs Firouz mounted an expedition to try and discover more, and she did find a few small herds living wild and preyed on by wolves. A few were captured and sent to the royal stables of Iran. Mrs Firouz also checked villages and towns, often on horseback or on foot as the roads were so poor. She found fifty animals with definite Caspian characteristics.

In 1972 a stallion and mare were presented to the Duke of Edinburgh to establish a stud here in Britain. But in 1977 the Royal Horse Society of Iran declared a ban on exports of Caspian Horses to save them from extinction, and established a national stud specially for them. There are probably about eighty horses now in Iran. Before this, studs had been started in Bermuda, America, Australia, New Zealand, Venezuela and Britain. There are five studs here with about forty Caspians in all.

The Caspian stands from 9-12 hands, averaging about 11.2 h.h. They grow very quickly and have made all their height by two years old. They have an Arab head with small, pointed, turned-in ears, large eyes and low-set nostrils. They are long in the leg, with a very fine, narrow, dense, cannon bone. They have the action of a thoroughbred rather than the knee-type action of a pony, and their immensely strong, narrow little feet, never need shoeing.

Quiet, confident and sensible, but powerful for its size and with an extraordinary jumping ability, it makes a perfect child's pony or driving pony.

Let's hope it will survive and emulate the Arab to become a breed of international repute, for although its star is rising 300 years later than the Arab's, it is the older breed by 3000 years.

Left: Amu Daria, a true Caspian. It is hard to believe that this stallion is under 12h.h.

Above: Maroun, a six-year-old bay Caspian stallion, receiving his prize at the Mid-Shires Show in 1978.

A Visit to Norman Thelwell

Norman Thelwell, better known simply as Thelwell, has probably had more fun out of horses and ponies than anyone else I can think of. He lives in a beautiful part of Hampshire, and it's here that he does the drawings that have been making people laugh for years.

As I walked up to his house, there in a paddock, stood a little fat pony. Was this the inspiration for the famous 'Kipper', perhaps the best known and best loved little pony in the world?

Then there at the door, a small, dark, rather serious man, with a faint Liverpool accent and twinkling eyes.

'I'm not a great rider, you know,' he began. 'I believe horses are dangerous at both ends and uncomfortable in the middle. I go to horse shows, but just as a member of the public. I like to stand on the sidelines and watch, because I think that if you're on a horse being bucked about you can't really see what is happening but if you're watching someone else going through it you can pick up more.'

As I find horses hard to draw I wondered if he had had any training.

'Not specifically to draw horses, no. But I can't remember a time in my life when I didn't draw, and I like all animals and birds, but I draw more horses than anything. They're beautiful; they're beautiful to paint and very likable things to have around.'

Did he do a lot of research for his books?

'Yes. First you have to decide what kind of book you are going to do. For example, I did a book on Western riding and I filled maybe three or four books with notes. Next, the drawings have to be accurate so I make many drawings of any details I might need. I have a fair knowledge of what a Western saddle is like, but every Western saddle is not the same and I must know in what ways they differ, for instance, a Mexican saddle is different from those used further north. Also important is the decoration on saddles and boots and the clothes they wear.

'People in this country are very knowledgeable about cowboys and the West because of the thousands of Westerns they have seen on television and at the cinema. It's no good just making jokes and drawing funny pictures; it's all got to be very authentic.'

But where did he get all this information?

'Well, I get books on the subject from wherever necessary. For the Western book I got a lot from the United States and then I visited the Flying 'G' Ranch, which is a Western-style stables in the New Forest, and made drawings from the actual saddlery. I had to find out a lot about the rules of the various competitions that cowboys go in for as well. For instance, in American rodeos you can ride with a saddle or you can ride bareback, where you just hold on to a sort of handle on the cinch, or you can even ride a bull.

'I also discovered that a friendly horse can be a great disadvantage, at least in a rodeo. You get more points if you get a really nasty one.'

But where did all the ideas come from?

'From a number of sources. Going to shows and drawing from life, by looking at books and photographs and also from the television. I saw your round at

Did I *really* look like that?

Olympia and that immediately gave me an idea.'

And the little fat pony and its owner, where did they come from?

'Well some years ago I was drawing mainly country subjects for Punch magazine, principally because I am very interested in the English countryside. It just so happened that on one occasion I made a drawing with a pony in it, simply because a pony is very much part of the English countryside. We had an immediate reaction from the readers and a lot of letters, so I tried another drawing with a pony in it, with the same result. The strange thing was that whenever I did a pony we always got a lot of letters. Eventually the editor rang me and asked if I could do a double-page spread on this subject. Well, quite honestly, I can remember panicking and saying, "I've drained the subject dry; I've done three already." But the

Just four pages from the notebooks which Norman Thelwell filled with sketches before starting work on his Western riding book.

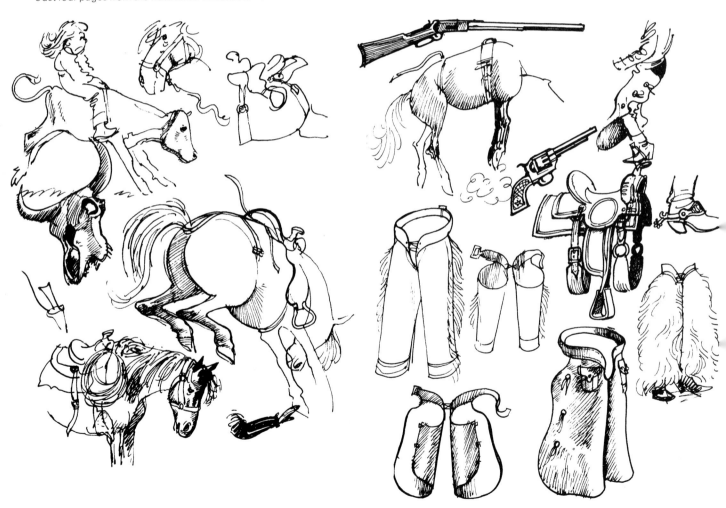

editor said, "Have a go"; so I did and in a way the ponies have simply taken over since then. People seem to like them all over the world – behind the Iron Curtain, Japan, America, and so on. I'm very pleased but I'm still not quite sure why they've taken off in the way they have.'

Was there ever a real Penelope and Kipper ?

'Yes. My daughter's name is Penelope and she had a pony called Kipper. He was just about as fat and round as you can possibly get and had this long mane, so that you could rarely see his eyes. You had to move his mane to check whether he was asleep or awake.'

He seems able to find something funny in everything.

'Yes, but in fact I'm not making any jokes in these books. I'm writing what is basically a correct instruction manual. All I do is interpret each detail of the instruction in my own particular way. That's where, I hope, the humour lies. In other words, if you were to take away all the drawings and bring all the text together it would be a simple manual on how one ought to deal with ponies.'

33

Tack Cleaning

Cleaning equipment and products : neatsfoot oil, soft cloth, Kocholine, oil, sponge, saddle soap and metal polish.

If you have your own horse or pony you will want to know how to care for all that valuable tack it wears.

Keeping your tack in tip-top condition will prolong its life and make for safer riding – and it looks smarter too.

Always make sure that your saddle is clean. Use saddle soap and warm soapy water to clean it and then give it a good polish with a soft cloth.

The stirrup irons should be removed from the leathers and, if dirty, washed in soapy water. When they are dry give them a good rub with a dry duster.

Wash, dry and then saddle soap the stirrup leathers. After you have dried them off always check for signs of cracking. Stirrup leathers, along with the girth, are the most important things on a saddle – if they break while you are riding you could be in trouble. If they are dry rub in either a small amount of neatsfoot oil or try 'Kocholine', which is a sort of red-coloured jelly very good for making leather more supple.

As for the girths, the same methods of cleaning apply. Of course, don't saddle soap your girths if they are made of

webbing ! When hanging a girth up to dry never hang from just one end, always hang from both, in a 'U' shape. This is particularly important with nylon girths. If a girth hangs from one end only, water runs to the bottom end and acts on the steel buckles creating acid which will rot the nylon holding the buckle.

Always check buckles, particularly those of the stirrup leathers. If they become very worn and flat, it is a good idea to ask your saddler to replace them.

Stiff buckles can be made less so by oiling them with a light machine oil. Move the buckle to and fro to enable the oil to penetrate.

Make a special point of checking and oiling the safety catch on the stirrup bars. It must open easily in case of an emergency and if it has become stiff it will not do its job properly. Its function is to hold the stirrup leather until extra pressure is put on it (such as when a rider's foot gets caught up in the stirrup during a fall). When this happens the stirrup leather must come away freely from the bar to avoid injury to the rider.

The method of cleaning bridles, martingales and head collars is similar to that used for the saddle. First, take each item to pieces, always checking for signs of worn leather or buckles.

Wash the bridle all over in soapy water, and include the bit. Check the bit carefully for any

Wash stirrup irons in warm soapy water then rub with a dry cloth.

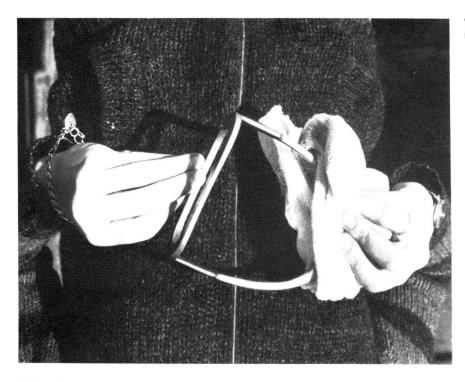

Below: Check stirrup-leather buckles for signs of wear. Make sure they are neither too loose nor too stiff.

Buckles which are stiff can be easily loosened with a drop of light oil.

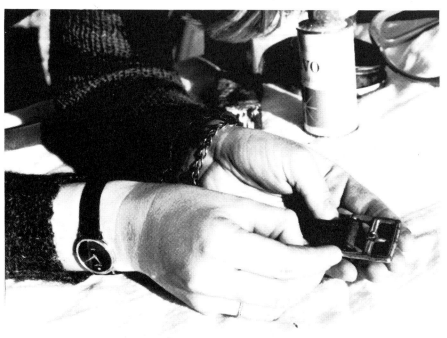

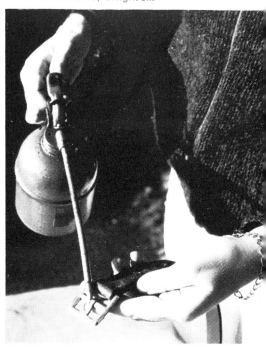

signs of worn or rough edges as these could injure the horse's mouth.

Once the bridle has dried off, and this can be done by using a chamois leather, rub in saddle soap with a cloth held firmly between your fingers and thumb.

If the reins are dry rub in some neatsfoot oil using a cloth. Reins should be checked regularly for signs of cracking.

Buckles on martingales, bridles headcollars and saddles can all be cleaned with metal polish. This is not necessary for every cleaning session when a rub with a dry duster is usually enough to restore the shine.

A stud-billeted bridle is easier to clean than a stitched one, but check the stud billets regularly to make sure they are not becoming loose. When you have undone the bridle, open out the folds and, after cleaning, rub in plenty of saddle soap. The

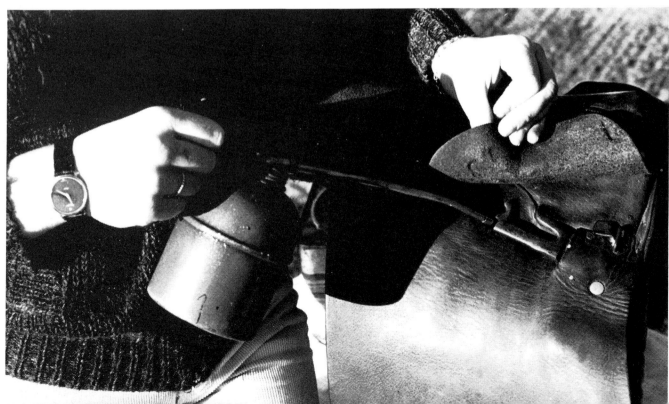

leather here must be supple. Not only will this minimise the wear and tear but it will make it easier to undo.

When you've finished cleaning your tack, always hang or support it properly to prevent it from mis-shaping (which would be a pity after all your hard work!).

Top left: To clean a bridle properly, you must first take it to pieces.

Top right: Wash the bit in soapy water and rub dry with a soft cloth. Check for rough edges, as these could damage your pony's mouth.

Bottom left: Reins can be saddle soaped and allowed to dry.

Bottom right: Cracked reins will benefit from treatment with neatsfoot oil or Kocholine. Rub in well and allow to dry. Reins *must* be kept in good condition.

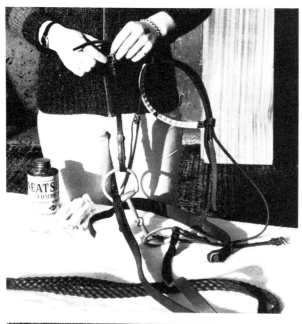

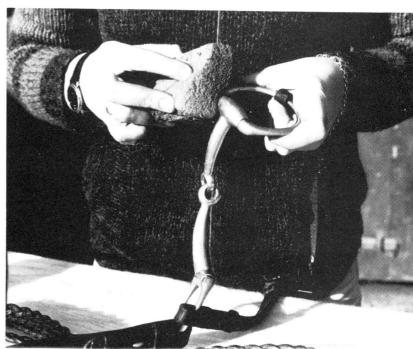

POLO

If you suddenly found yourself galloping flat out on your pony so that you deliberately collided with another pony and rider, you would probably be playing polo.

Polo is the fastest, roughest team game in the world, and the oldest. Half the joy of the game is that it's a body-contact sport, with a lot of 'riding-off'.

It's rather like hockey on horseback. Each team consists of four players. Numbers 1 and 2 are the forwards, number 3 is the half-back, and number 4 the back. Each member of the team marks his opposite number, and each has a handicap ranging from —2 to + 10 goals. The handicaps of all four players are added together to give the team handicap. If, for instance, team A has a total handicap of 8 and team B a handicap of 6, team B will start with a 2-goal advantage, as the team with the higher handicap concedes to the other team the difference between the two handicaps so that they are fairly matched.

There is a mounted referee and two mounted umpires. The game is played on a 'ground' 300 yards × 200 yards. The goal posts are 10 feet high and 24 feet apart.

It's a game of great skill and is played at amazing speed. A full game consists of six 'chukkas' (rounds), each one lasting 7 minutes. There are intervals of 3 minutes between chukkas, and 5 minutes at half time. To ensure fairness the teams change ends every time a goal is scored. Ponies normally play two chukkas in an afternoon, with a rest of at least one chukka in between.

Polo was played in Persia as long ago as 500 BC in the reign of Darius I, and later spread east to China and Japan where it became the national game. It also became very popular in India where the British army discovered it and brought it back to this country about a hundred years ago. Today it is very popular in Argentina, America and India.

There isn't such a thing as a breed of polo pony. They're

Polo today – little change over the centuries.

either large ponies or small horses. What's wanted is an animal with speed and the ability to turn on a sixpence. It must have the right temperament and a good mouth. The ability to stop and turn at break-neck speed is vital because it can win or lose a match.

People who say that polo ponies have mouths like iron can only have ridden the really bad type of polo pony. In fact, it's absolutely impossible to be a good player and ride a pony with a bad mouth. Firstly because you have to be able to stop them quickly, and secondly because they are ridden with one hand only and are schooled to

neck-rein. As the rider moves his hand across to the right, the pony turns right in response to the touch of the rein on the left side of its neck, and vice versa.

At first the height of the ponies was limited to 14 h.h., then that was increased to 14.2 h.h. and there are ponies playing in England up to 15.3 h.h. But whatever the size of the pony, the closer you are to the ground, the easier it is to hit the ball.

Ninety per cent of the polo ponies in this country have been imported from the Argentine, where they can play polo for twelve months of the year. There are hundreds and hundreds of horses on the pampas and

Left: The ancient game of polo. An illustration from a Persian manuscript of 1480 AD.

ranches, and the Argentinians are good breakers and makers of horses, spending hours of patient unhurried work making a new horse.

The ponies have their manes shorn, for if you have to move the stick quickly over the horse's neck you don't want to get caught up in the mane. A mane can also be very sharp and could cut your fingers badly.

The tail is plaited down into one big plait, then done up with a tail bandage. There are certain shots when the player has to lean right back and if he got the stick underneath the horse's tail the natural reaction for the horse would be to clamp its tail down, and the player wouldn't be able to get the stick out for the next shot. There are also other shots where the player has to lean out and could actually hit the tail if the horse is swishing it about.

Great care is taken of the pony's legs in all its work and training, and the legs are always bandaged for a game. The bandages serve two purposes. When you're galloping at about 25 miles an hour and you ask a horse to stop or turn suddenly this puts a tremendous strain and pressure on the tendons. So the bandages give the legs extra support. Also, because polo is a fairly violent game and there are sticks flying everywhere, they protect the horses' legs from both the stick and the ball.

The bridle has an ordinary noseband and a simple bit like a short-cheek Pelham, or an Argentinian bit or a vulcanite bit, all of which are very kind to the pony. They all usually have rubber rings at the corners of the mouth ; this is terribly important

as all that violent activity could otherwise make the corners of the mouth very sore.

The ponies wear a martingale and a breast plate. The latter is not normally used in riding but is necessary on the polo ground because there is so much movement in the saddle. It stops the saddle slipping back and giving the pony a sore back. A surcingle is put right over the saddle to keep it absolutely firm on the horse's back, so that if the girth should break, because of all that movement in the saddle, it will act as a second girth.

The worst fall a rider can have is if a girth should break when he's galloping at 25 mph. In fact, it isn't the horses that get injured, it's the riders. Polo ponies are valuable animals and certainly, the percentage of injured horses in polo is no more than in eventing, show-jumping or racing.

Nor is it any longer a game played only by the super-rich. Four of the present English polo team came from the Pony Club and more and more Pony Club branches are taking it up. And girls can play too !

Superb action, typical of a good polo pony.

HORSE SENSE

One of the things that my father, who has worked with horses all his life, has always taught me, is that a great deal of the need for first aid can be avoided with good management and common sense.

When you have at last persuaded your parents that the time has come to buy a pony, do try to buy a really healthy one.

This may sound very obvious but many people find themselves with a lot of heartbreak after buying an animal they felt sorry for, or after buying the first one they saw.

So remember, keep a cool head and make a thorough nuisance of yourself. Ask to see the pony ridden in traffic, as a

traffic-shy one is both frightening and dangerous. Ask to see him caught, and if possible led in and out of a trailer. Ask if he has any particular likes and dislikes – any genuine pony owner will be anxious that the pony is going to a good, caring home where he will be happy.

Having satisfied yourself that

Properly managed, a grass-kept pony should remain in first-class condition all the year round.

A clear, bright eye is a sure sign of good health.

pony out. First, the fencing. The post and rail type is the best, but very expensive. Posts and plain wire is a good substitute, but the wire must be taut and the posts firmly set. Loose or barbed wire can be very dangerous and is just asking for trouble as ponies can get their legs caught up and badly injured.

Make sure the gate is stout and shuts securely – you would be surprised at how deftly some ponies can undo gate latches.

Walk over your field and check for broken glass, tin cans, plastic litter and pot holes, all of which can be the cause of you having a sick pony on your hands. Learn to recognise poisonous plants so that you can remove and burn them. Don't just pull them up and leave them in the field, as they are often more dangerous in their half-wilted state. A few common ones are the bright yellow ragwort, deadly nightshade, and yew. Also, acorns in excess should be removed.

A good shelter is important, and can be simply constructed, to protect your pony from wind and rain in winter, and flies in summer. A good water supply is essential. You should use a heavy container that your pony can't knock over, and one which has no sharp edges. It should sit flat on the ground so there is no danger of your pony getting a foot trapped under it. Keep the container spotlessly clean, and freshly filled. In very cold weather you will have to break the ice for your pony as he can't do this himself.

In winter your pony should not get cold, provided he has good food, good hay, shelter and plenty of water. You should visit

you are capable of riding the pony and that you are happy with each other, you should get a vet to inspect him. Although this will cost quite a lot, it is a very worthwhile investment. There are lots of things that even the most experienced horseman cannot tell from just looking at a pony and your vet will possibly be the best friend you and your pony can have.

Most ponies, and certainly our own native breeds, can live out all the year round, but a few simple rules must be observed. You must inspect your field carefully before turning your

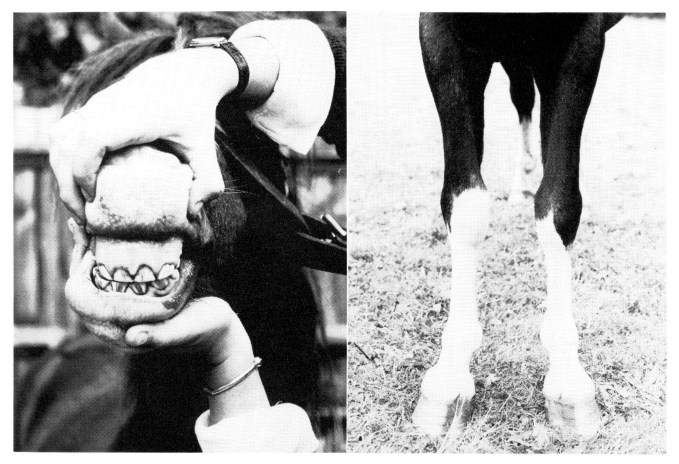

Check your horse's mouth regularly for sharp or jagged teeth. Ask your farrier or vet to file down any rough edges.

Good, clean legs – no bumps or lumps.

him at least twice a day, and catch him up at least once for a closer look. Don't groom him too much if he is living out, just remove any caked mud. Lots of brushing will remove the natural oils which he needs to keep out the damp and the cold. Pick out, oil, and inspect his feet every day. In very muddy conditions you can wash the feet, but only if you take great care to dry them thoroughly. If you see any small cracks appearing in the bulb of the heel at the back of the foot, you should wash and dry the area carefully and apply a good antiseptic cream. If the trouble persists, consult your vet.

During the summer, the most common ailment is simply over-eating, so keep a careful eye on your pony's waistline. Laminitis, which is a painful inflammation inside the hoof, can be caused by an excess of rich fresh grass and insufficient exercise, and often affects our native pony breeds. If you think your pony is getting too fat try and bring him into a stable during the day to cut down on his eating hours. If this is not possible, perhaps you could confine him to a small area of his field (including the shelter) and try to give him more exercise. If he does get laminitis, he will be in great pain and appear rooted to the spot, showing great reluctance to move. You should call the vet immediately if you suspect laminitis.

Apart from checking his feet daily yourself, you should also arrange for a farrier to come regularly, about every six weeks, to trim his feet and check or replace his shoes. Your pony will also need to be wormed at

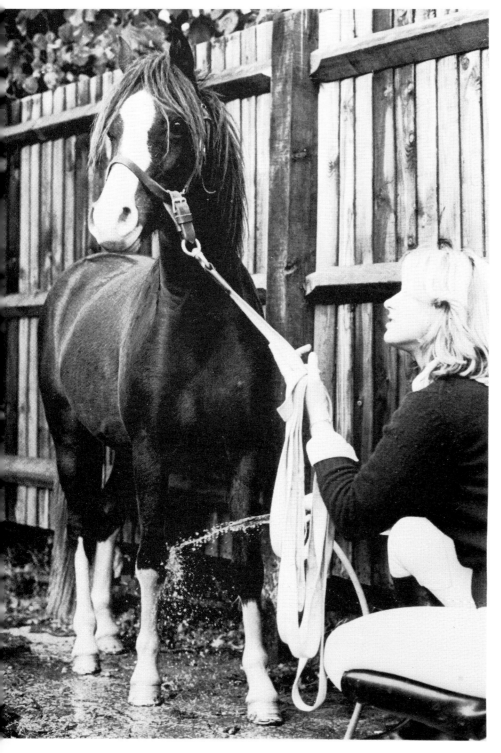

regular intervals throughout the year and you should take your vet's advice about this. Also, make sure that his anti-flu and anti-tetanus injections are up to date.

The grass in the field can be kept healthy and sweet by removing droppings as often as possible, and by harrowing and topping the grass – if you are in doubt about this, ask for help from a friendly farmer. The reason you need to do this is that horses and ponies are very choosy about which type of grass they eat, and do not like the long, tough tufts of grass which tend to grow around old droppings. If at all possible the field should be rested from time to time to prevent it becoming 'horse-sick'. And remember to keep checking for dangerous plants, and litter, and also make a habit of checking the fencing from time to time.

It is very useful to keep a small first-aid kit handy, containing antiseptic liquid, cream or spray; clean dressings for minor cuts and scratches; cotton wool; scissors with blunt ends; and bandages to cover larger wounds until your vet arrives. But always remember that prevention is better than cure, so the more you visit, examine, and talk to your pony and know how he looks when he is healthy, the sooner you will be able to spot if he has any problems. That way trouble is nipped in the bud. But always, if in doubt, call the vet.

If you suspect swelling or heat in the legs, hosing down with cold water can be very beneficial.

Tethering

You are lucky indeed if finding grazing for your pony is not a problem. But did you know that there are lots of commons and open spaces around where you are allowed to graze a pony, providing it is tethered? It's worth finding out about these areas as they can offer good alternative grazing when your pony's normal grazing has to be rested. A phone call to your local council offices is all that should be needed.

However, you must know how to tether a pony properly, or you and your pony will soon be in all sorts of trouble.

Unless you know for certain that your pony has been tethered before (and never believe what the previous owner has told you), you can't simply take him out onto an open space, tether him and expect everything to be all right. It won't be. Also, it is unlikely that an old horse or pony will take to being tethered if introduced to it too late in life. So proceed with caution.

Well, what do you need and how do you start? First, you need a neck strap. It must be strong and broad, about 2 inches wide, with a sturdy 'D' ring for a chain. It's very important that the strap is pliable, so keep it nice and soft with oil or it will chafe the pony's neck. It must fit comfortably, but make sure it won't slip off over his head, or that if he should scratch with his back leg he won't

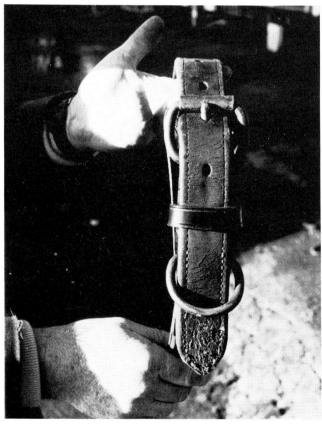

The neck strap must be strong, with secure buckles and keepers. The leather should be supple so as not to chafe the pony's neck.

You also need a good, strong link chain which has a swivel to prevent the chain from twisting and knotting.

get his foot caught. Never tether in a halter ; it is too easily broken.

Next, you require a chain, not too heavy for the pony to manage, but strong enough to hold him. Make sure the links are not worn. Twenty to twenty-five feet is a good length and it should have a swivel and clip on the end to fasten onto the 'D' ring on the neck strap. The swivel will prevent the chain from twisting and 'locking up'. Never use rope, nylon or otherwise, as it will twist into knots and get tangled round the pony's legs.

Lastly, you need a good strong peg or metal stake, at least 3 feet long. This should also have a ring and swivel on it.

It's vital that these three items are strong and in good order. Never try to save money by 'making do' – you'll end up with your pony missing and possibly the cause of a nasty accident.

Before you take your pony out to the grazing, you must get him used to wearing a neck strap and to the noise of the chain. If he has a stable, let him wear the strap and chain in his box until you feel he's relaxed with them. Then take him out and let him walk around in a small paddock or yard until he learns how to manage his feet and the chain. Until he knows how to do this it's much safer to take his shoes off, in case they get caught in the chain and he panics.

Now he has to get used to actually being tethered. For safety try this in your own field. It will take about a fortnight for him to adjust to the chain and its restrictions. Always keep the chain the same length, and leave his head collar or halter on to start with.

Once you are ready to take him out you will have to decide where you are going to tether him. Obviously it must be a spot that has nice grazing, but make sure he can't reach any plants or bushes that are poisonous, and remember he can stretch his neck further than you might think. He should be able to find some shelter from the wind and hot sun. Make sure he can't get caught up and twisted round old tree stumps or small bushes and don't tether him so that his chain crosses a footpath or someone may have a nasty accident.

When you have tethered him, stay with him till he is settled, checking the neck strap is safe and comfortable. Visit him at least every morning and every

The steel peg must be long enough to obtain a good hold in the ground.

evening to see that he's all right and to take him fresh water. Move him when necessary to a fresh spot and, most important of all, in bad weather bring him in.

Nobody pretends that tethering a pony is the ideal, but properly managed you'll find your pony will benefit from the extra grazing when you are short.

Once you have satisfied yourself that everything has been checked, you can leave your pony to graze happily.

The Golden Horseshoe Ride

On the ride. Competitors cross one of the many streams on the Moor.

Have you ever been long-distance riding ? Well I have and it is not something I wish to do again in a hurry !

The ride I took part in was the 'Golden Horseshoe' long-distance ride over Exmoor. It covered a distance of 75 miles which had to be completed within two days ; 50 miles the first day and 25 miles the next. But before I recount my experiences, let me tell you something about this sport, which is becoming more and more popular among riders all over the country.

Long-distance riding is for anyone, provided that both you and even more important, your horse, are properly prepared. The challenge is in building up the fitness of the horse. The ride is a test of endurance and stamina and it really does take months before you are ready to attempt such a ride.

The British Horse Society's Long-Distance Riding Group operates in the same way as other equestrian groups administered from the National Equestrian Centre at Stoneleigh, and the sport itself is now both nationally and internationally recognised.

It is not a new sport. The first long-distance ride organised in this country took place in about 1912. But the first actual Golden

Horseshoe ride was staged in 1965, when 120 entrants took part. The following year, qualifying rides were held and 81 reached the final. Since then the numbers who have taken part in qualifying rounds have grown, in fact, so much so, that organisers have limited the number taking part in the final to approximately 70.

The enjoyment of such a ride comes from the chance to ride over long stretches of countryside. Skill is needed too, as riders have to judge their speed carefully, aiming at an average of 8 mph. The halfway check-in includes a vet's inspection, and if your horse does not come up to necessary standards of fitness, you are not allowed to carry on. At the end of the second half – the return journey – your horse has to undergo another rigorous vet's inspection.

It was decided that I should take part only in the second day's ride as I was not a regular rider and probably not up to doing the whole ride. At the time, I thought I was perfectly capable but what a shock I had coming to me!

As I had come all the way from London, someone who lived in the village of Exford, in Exmoor, supplied my horse. It had been hunted through the season and was therefore in fairly good condition and well able to stand the 25 miles that I was to ride.

And so the ride set off, starting at eight in the morning, the riders leaving at four-minute intervals. I left at about 8.30, and as I waved goodbye to the film crew, I had no idea what I had let myself in for!

The crew were to catch up with me at certain points along the route to see how I was getting on and to talk to me. But because I would have to pace my speed, I would not have time to stop and talk so I was fitted with a radio mike and battery so that they could hear me the whole time. Well, that was the first big mistake. After a while, the battery, which was fitted onto the saddle by my knee, began to rub my leg. And after the first couple of miles I began to see how fortunate I was that I hadn't persuaded them to let me ride both days!

My whole body ached!

Obviously because of lack of riding experience and proper body positioning my back was killing me! It felt as though the bones in my bottom were coming right through my skin, and I tried to ride with my bottom out of the saddle. My arms ached and my shoulder muscles felt as though they were about to give way! Honestly, I was well and truly finished by the time I got back.

It was late morning when I arrived at the finish and my first thought was for a drink. I was dying of thirst and I must have downed about two pints of lager (ugh!).

Not having been a proper entrant, obviously I was not placed, but did receive a rosette for taking part.

It was a great experience, looking back, but at the time all I could think about was the agony I was in. So be warned: never compete in anything like this unless you have had the proper training and built up to it. Don't be like me and think you can do it just because it's simply a ride – when I got off that horse I could hardly move a muscle! Never again.

OUR RECORD BREAKER

The first coach to be seen in England is said to have been brought from the town of Kotje in Hungary during the reign of Queen Elizabeth I.

The first mail coach service was started in 1784 by John Palmer of Bath. Up to that time, mail was carried on horseback by post-boys who were easily attacked and robbed. The mail coaches were much safer and quickly became popular because they could carry up to nine passengers. An inside seat cost 5 pence a mile and a seat on top cost half that.

In 1815, after Telford and MacAdam had solved the problem of the atrocious road surfaces, hundreds of coaches appeared on the roads.

Stage coaches were built like mail coaches but could carry

You can see why the coachman's horn became known as the Yard of Tin.

Mr Mossman's record-breaking team in action, seconds after the coach has come to a halt.

more passengers on top, up to twelve. On the mail coaches the space at the back had to be reserved for the guard in charge of the mail bags; on the stage coach this provided space for another eight passengers.

The mail coaches were always finished in royal colours: black with maroon panels with the royal cypher and scarlet wheels and undercarriage. Stage coaches were painted in brilliant colours with the names of their stopping places painted in bold letters. They also carried a red-coated guard whose job it was to sound

the horn, guard the passengers' luggage and keep the coachman up to time.

The coach-horn that the guards used to give warning of their approach was usually made of brass or tin and was about three feet long. It became known affectionately as a Yard of Tin.

The guards developed special calls to identify the coaches as they approached and also to give warning of what they wanted at the stop. The most famous calls were 'Clear the road', and of course 'Tally-ho' which came from the well-known coach of

that name; and there were other calls like 'Lame Horse' and 'Change Horses'.

The mail coach had complete right of way over everything and everybody on the road, a right which was put to the test in a nasty incident when a mail coach drove straight through a troop of soldiers who didn't get off the road.

I tried blowing a coach horn and it's not easy. You have to imagine that you've got a hair on the tip of your tongue and try to spit it off, as you mouth the words of the call.

was then known as 'Old Times' and now belongs to Mr Bernard Mills. It has been renamed the 'Selby' coach after James Selby the coachman who won that bet by completing the journey with ten minutes to spare.

There were twelve staging posts on each leg of the journey, but in fact Selby stopped at only seven on each journey. So the horses were changed fourteen times and only one change took more than a minute, and two changes were made in 47 seconds.

But all these records were broken in 1963 when Mr Sanders Watney, then President of the British Driving Society, decided to see if he could train a team of grooms to make a change of horses even more quickly. And he did, setting a new record time of 45 seconds.

This is where we came into the story. The idea had caught the imagination of our producer and he asked Mr George Mossman if he would like to make an attempt at the record which we would film for the programme.

Mr Mossman was very enthusiastic and gathered together a team of 'grooms', all of whom are well known in their own right in the horse world – Pat Cooke, Christine and John Dick, and Peter and Ann Munt.

To show that it wasn't as easy as it might look, David Turnbull, our producer, decided that I should get a team of grooms together and have a go as well.

It was all to take place at The Five Bells o' Stanbridge one cold March morning, and Mr Sanders Watney agreed to act as judge and official time-keeper.

The time was to run from the

In the 1830s, when the railways started up, many mail and stage coaches went off the road for ever, but in the brief fifteen years that were their hey-day they achieved such astonishing times and distances and feats of driving that they will never be forgotten.

As you can imagine, no one team of horses ever pulled a stage coach at speed with twelve passengers and their luggage on board, over any great distance. In fact the horses had to be changed about every fifteen miles at what were known as staging posts, most of which were at inns.

As soon as the grooms or ostlers heard the coach approaching, and the guard blowing his horn, they would get the next team ready to make the change so that the coach could be on its way again as soon as possible.

A hundred years ago the Brighton Coach used to make the sixty-mile journey between Piccadilly in London and The Old Ship Inn in Brighton every day, taking six hours.

In 1888 a famous wager was laid for a thousand pounds that the Brighton Coach could not be driven from Piccadilly to Brighton and back in eight hours.

The actual coach that was used

moment the wheels of the coach came to a stop to when they turned and moved off again, and Mr Watney had brought the 'Selby' coach, the actual coach that won that amazing wager, nearly a hundred years ago, and it looked as good as new.

Mr Mossman's team explained to us how to manage the horses, uncouple the reins, and traces, pull out the leaders and then the wheel horses, and how to re-hitch the second team and fasten the reins again. It seemed impossible that we could do it in anything like the time. The horses behaved beautifully but we were all fingers and thumbs. We certainly weren't favourites to break the record but we were determined to have a go.

As we heard the coach arriving and the guard blowing his horn, the time keepers looked to their watches. Suddenly the horses were there and we were off. The coachman threw down his reins and we flung ourselves at the horses. 'Now your rein . . . outside traces on . . . give the other rein over . . . watch that coupling . . . right . . . the other horse . . . ooh, he's eaten my button hole! . . . that's it, out of the way . . . drive on!

It took us 1 minute 45 seconds. Now it was Mr Mossman's turn. Having tried it myself I knew just how difficult it was. Would his team really be able to make the change in less than 45 seconds?

Well, they did. They completed the change in an astonishing 41 seconds – a new record.

LONDON, 10 O'CLOCK.	M.	Arr.	Dep.
STREATHAM *Changed in 47 sec.*	7	10 28	10 29
CROYDON *Passed through*	11		
PURLEY BOTTOM *Changed, 1 min. 5 sec.*	14½	10 57	10 58½
MERSTHAM *Plate greased & changed 2 m.*	20	11 27	11 29
HORLEY *Changed Horses in 55 sec.*	26	11 51½	11 52½
CRAWLEY *Ran through*	31	12 11	
PEAS POTTAGE *Changed, 1 min. 2 sec.*	33	12 23½	12 25
HANDCROSS *Ran through*	35	12 33½	
CUCKFIELD *Changed in 1 min. 8 sec.*	40	12 53½	12 54½
FRIAR'S OAK *Changed in 1 min.*	45	1 17	
PATCHAM *Changed in 47 sec.*	50	1 40	1 41
SHIP, BRIGHTON *Turned round*	54	1 56	

BRIGHTON, 1.56 O'CLOCK.	M.	Arr.	Dep.
THE KENNELS *Comp. got down for 1st time*	5	2 17½	2 20
FRIAR'S OAK *Changed horses, greased plate*	9	2 35	2 36
CUCKFIELD	14	2 54	2 55
HANDCROSS	19	3 21½	
PEAS POTTAGE *Changed in 1 min.*	21	3 29	3 30
CRAWLEY *Passed through*	23		
HORLEY *Changed in 56 sec.*	28	3 57½	3 58½
RED HILL *Turned corner galloping*	32	4 12	
MERSTHAM *Greased plate again*	34	4 24	4 25
PURLEY BOTTOM *Changed 50 sec.*	39½	4 51	4 52
CROYDON *Right through*	43		
STREATHAM *Changed, 55 sec.*	47	5 20	5 21
PICCADILLY *Cheers*	54	5 50	

COACH MATCH AGAINST TIME

THE GALLOPING STAGE, "OLD TIMES," PASSING LOWFIELD HEATH, PACE 20 MILES AN HOUR

On July 13th, 1888, the Brighton Coach, "Old Times," was driven from the White Horse Cellars to Brighton and back for the wager of £1,000 to £500 against it being accomplished in 8 hours. The road was cleared in front of the starting place, and the veteran whip, James Selby, gave orders to "Let go" at 10 o'clock precisely. The Coach arrived at The Old Ship Brighton, 1-56"-10', having accomplished the journey just under 4 hours. The stay at Brighton was momentary, the horses were merely turned round; ultimately the Coach arrived at Piccadilly, at 5.50, or 10 minutes under the stipulated time, and 40 minutes within the record.

The occupants of the Coach were J. W. Selby (Whip), H. L. Beckett, Carleton Blyth, A. S. Broadwood, William P. Cosier, A. F. McAdam, W. J. Godden (Guard).

The Gathering

Wales is a land of ponies. Wherever you go, you see them – in fields, on farms, and most of all covering those bleak Welsh Mountains – hence the Welsh Mountain pony.

As many of you may have guessed, the Welsh pony is my favourite breed, Cusop being one of them! The Welsh Mountain pony has been bred on the hills of Wales since the days of the Romans. Since then there have been infusions of Arab, thoroughbred and even hackney blood, and this gives us the breed as we know it today.

There are four different types

of Welsh pony : Section A, which is limited to 12 h.h. ; Section B, which must not exceed 13.2 h.h. and is of fine quality, suitable for riding ; Section C, which also must not exceed 13.2 h.h. and has more of a cob-type appearance, in other words is slightly heavier built ; and finally Section D, usually standing from 14.2-15 h.h. and known as the Welsh Cob.

The Section A ponies are very pretty ; they have very fine heads with slightly dished profiles, large bold eyes, and ears which are pricked and pert. They are very hardy and sound little ponies and have true pony action and character. Any other pony would probably not survive the climate of the Welsh hills, especially in winter, but to the Section A it is no problem. Once tamed, they are extremely gentle yet at the same time courageous. They are absolutely ideal for breeding quality show ponies, and because they are so strong and versatile, they make ideal ride and drive ponies. So many Pony Club ponies seem to be Section A. This is probably because they are so nippy and quick. The colours vary from chestnut, brown, bay, black, dun, cream, to grey.

My chance to have a good look at the Welsh Mountain pony came when I visited Gwyn Price at his home in Wales. He was having a round-up along with several of his neighbours, to sort out some ponies to be sold at a nearby auction. It was a marvellous chance to see these ponies in their natural surroundings and something which I have always wanted to do. I don't think I have ever had such a fantastic time as when I rode over the mountains

there on horseback. Mind you, it was extremely cold and I felt very aware of the elements, particularly being so high above sea-level.

Gwyn Price has been breeding horses and ponies for years, and on this particular mountain he had about 200 ponies ! In fact his grandfather and great-grandfather had bred ponies on these same mountains before him.

Gwyn is a judge of the Welsh breeds and was therefore able to tell me quite a bit about them. The Section B is the riding pony among the breeds. He is very similar to the smaller 'A' but has a riding quality about him with a good action. Strong limbs and a tail set high and carried well are essentials.

Section Cs should be the same height as the Bs but of a much heavier build and more thickly set. He is very versatile, combining strength with quality and common sense. They are still used on a great many farms for shepherding – they are just the right size for getting on and off to open gates, or for slipping off quickly if you want to catch, say, a sheep. Better all round really, because they can carry a pretty hefty rider, too.

The Section C makes a good ride and drive pony. He is a very sturdy animal with powerful hindquarters which makes him able to carry just that little bit more without undue strain. Around his heels he has just a little bit of 'feather', like the Welsh Cob.

The Section D, the Welsh Cob, is the biggest of the breeds. They stand on average 14.2 h.h. and over, but if they become too high, they tend to become rather horsy

and so lose their 'cobbiness'. Their ears are bold and pricked ; their eyes, too, are bold and fairly wide apart. Their limbs are strong and they have a great, fiery presence. They are extremely courageous and have plenty of

Welsh Cobs, now much sought-after, especially for driving.

action, which is perhaps what makes them so popular with the Welsh men. They can cover the ground at a fairly fast pace, and with tremendous power. They are very good under saddle and are also ideal for harness classes.

My day with Mr Price was very tiring but one which I certainly will not forget in a hurry. It took the whole day to get all the horses rounded up and brought down to the farm to be sorted out. Without the help of neighbours I don't think we would have managed it quite so easily. After the day's work, Mrs Price supplied us with an absolutely gorgeous tea and, having worked all day in the fresh mountain air, I was ravenous!

THE QUARTER HORSE

Today the Quarter Horse is regarded as the best 'cow-horse' there is. But curiously it was originally bred as a racehorse, and was the first breed to be actually developed in America. About 300 years ago, the principal sport in Virginia was 'match-racing'. The early settlers ran these two-horse races along village streets or lanes. So that everyone could see the start and the finish of the race, it was always run in a straight line and was seldom longer than a quarter of a mile. The horses became known as 'quarter-milers' and were soon being called 'quarter horses'.

Short-distance racing demands a brilliant performance. The horse has to make an 'explosive' start and reach full speed after the first stride. It must run the entire race, which is very short, at full throttle; and it must run straight and true.

The horses were originally crosses between the best Spanish horses brought by the Conquistadors and the new horses arriving from England with the settlers. It was a compact, muscular horse. With its elegant legs and massive, powerful hindquarters, it could 'dust the nose' of any other breed in a sprint.

The settlers gradually moved west, taking the Quarter Horse with them. But now he had to pull waggons and buggies, even ploughs for the pioneers; and, of

A Quarter Horse gets down to work.

course, he had to carry the preachers and speed the doctors who followed.

It wasn't long before the ranchers and cowboys recognised these horses as the best 'range horse' they'd ever seen. All over the West men paid good money for them and started to get rid of the difficult and semi-wild Mustangs that they were using.

The daily grind of range work was exhausting, especially in the summer heat and winter storms ; but the Quarter Horse seemed to be able to work all day without becoming leg-weary. Often they would work ten to fourteen hours a day and usually had to travel great distances in that time, and all this carrying a man and a heavy saddle.

The Western saddle is big, and comfortable – it had to be if a man was going to be able to spend a long day in the saddle. And you did sit *in* those saddles. Each saddle gradually shaped itself to fit not only its owner but also its horse, so that they both felt comfortable and secure.

Men swore by their saddles and considered it disgraceful to sell them. To say a man had 'sold his saddle' was as bad as saying he had sold his soul. Often a saddle would cost more than the horse, which gave rise to sayings like : 'There he goes with his $100 saddle and $10 horse.'

This type of saddle and style of riding was brought to Mexico by the Spaniards, who got it from the Moors, who in turn had learnt it from the Moslems some 1,200 years ago, in Morocco. The oldest known saddle, which was recovered deep-frozen from the tombs of Pazyryk in the Altai Mountains of western Siberia, where it had been buried since 430 BC, is exactly the same as the Mexican saddle used 2,000 years later.

The Western saddle had to be very strong and was purpose-built for the task in hand : the 'cutting' saddle had a deep seat and high cantle or back to give security in fast manoeuvres ;

The spotted Appaloosa, highly prized by the Nez Percé Indians.

the 'roping' saddle was flatter with a low cantle to enable the rider to dismount quickly. The strains involved in roping cattle are terrific and all sorts of different horns were designed for winding ropes around at the front of the saddle. If the rope slipped off you could lose a finger ; in fact, a lot of cowboys 'had a couple of fingers gone'. The saddles sometimes had 'bumpers' to protect the horse and rider from steers, and most were worn with a breast-plate or breast-collar so that cowboys could ride with a loose cinch (girth). That way they got a lot more work out of their horses. The saddles were ridden with several blankets underneath so that the horse was made more comfortable. But nevertheless the horse would be carrying 40 lbs of saddle plus 180 lbs of rider.

Cowboys always rode their horses with one hand, a style called 'neck-reining'. Here the horse responds to the lightest touch of the reins on its neck. If a bit was used at all it was simple and straight with short shanks, as a snaffle would cause a direct pull on the wrong side of the horse's mouth when the neck-rein was used.

It was in 'cutting' cattle that the Quarter Horse came into his own. Superbly balanced and collected, he could slide, turn, stop instantly and still keep his feet under him at all times. Like sheepdogs with sheep, Quarter Horses developed a 'cow sense' and are able to out-think and out-run the cattle, instinctively placing their rider in the best position to 'throw his loop'. When the rider dismounts, the horse keeps a tight rope on the animal until the tie is completed.

A Quarter Horse must be gentle, intelligent, powerfully muscled and 15.2-16.1 h.h. There are now four types : the working 'cow-horse' ; the pleasure horse for Western riding ; the halter or show horse ; and the racing horse, for the Quarter Horse has returned to where it began. More than a hundred tracks in America now hold Quarter Horse races. With its blazing speeds and photo finishes it has once again captured everyone's imagination, and it boasts the richest prize in racing : the All-American Futurity Stakes, worth more than a million dollars.

Probably the best all-round horse in the world, it is certainly the most popular. More than forty different countries have now imported it and there are more than a million registered in America.

THE APPALOOSA

The horse has transformed the way of life of many people, but nowhere did it do so more dramatically than in the Americas.

The story begins in Mexico over 450 years ago, when Hernando Cortés and the Spanish Conquistadors arrived in South America. Cortés had brought with him six stallions and seven mares. These were the first horses to be seen in America (if there were horses before this no one knew of them). As the conquest advanced, more horses followed. Inevitably, many were lost and others strayed. But many of the strays thrived, and by the 1800s huge herds roamed wild from Mexico right up to Canada.

At that time hundreds of different Indian tribes lived all over America. They seldom moved camp and when they did carried very little. Then it happened . . . the horse moving from the south and the west met the Indian of the plains, and the American Indian as we know him was 'born'. The dazzling, wild-riding, feathered-hunter of the plains on his painted war-horse had arrived. Now food and meat could be moved by the ton, buffalo could be hunted, tents could be bigger and tribes could gather from miles around. The men transformed themselves into hunters and warriors whose lives depended on horses. The capture of horses and pony herds became the prime purpose of raids on other tribes. A man's wealth and his tribe's were counted in horses.

These horses and ponies were called pintos. Pinto is not a breed of horse, however ; it is a type of colouring and marking. There are two specific types : the Piebald, which is black and white, and the Skewbald, which is brown and white.

The Indians specially prized these coloured horses, possibly

Appaloosa mare and foal.

because their markings helped to camouflage them, but probably because they could paint their mystic symbols on the white patches. The word 'pinto' comes from 'pintado', a Spanish word meaning painted.

These brave, rough, tough little ponies, the mongrels of the horse world, were in fact Mustangs. They also became the first cow-ponies, though ranchers quickly replaced them as soon as better horses could be found.

Today, the Mustang lives wild and free in specially protected areas as America's first and only wild horse.

But there is one other horse which will always be associated with the American Indian and which is more popular today than ever. The horse is the Appaloosa and the tribe which developed it was the Nez Percé.

The Nez Percés lived west of the Rockies in what is now Oregon, Washington and Idaho, on lands watered by the Palouse River. They were more skilful at breeding and handling horses than any other tribe and they bred a spotted horse renowned for its temperament, stamina and hardiness. They were called Palousies and eventually Appaloosas.

In May, 1877, after seventy-two years of peace, the Nez Percés suddenly found themselves at war with the white man, and the horse and the tribe were nearly lost forever. Their Chief, Young Joseph, decided to lead his people and their horses to safety in Canada, over a thousand miles away. The tribe numbered about five hundred, half of whom were women and children, and they took with them over two thousand of their magnificent Palousies.

A handful of warriors led the tribe and its horses through the Bitterroot Mountains, twice across the Rockies, through the Yellowstone (now a national park) and across the Missouri River. They were finally brought to a halt by their pursuers just thirty miles from the Canadian Line.

For 1,300 miles and four months they had outwitted and outfought the army units sent to stop them. Now only eighty-seven warriors faced the army. For two days on Bear Mountain they stood at bay, refusing to surrender. Then on the third day, 5th October, 1877 Chief Joseph spoke. 'Our Chiefs are killed; the old men are dead. The little children are freezing to death. Hear me, my Chiefs. I am tired; my heart is sick and sad. From where the sun now stands I will fight no more, forever.'

The army took the Indians' guns and killed their horses – the horses whose speed and stamina had made those Indians so formidable.

But somehow a few Nez Percés managed to escape to Canada and some horses did survive.

Sixty years later, in the late 1930s, the Appaloosa Horse Club was founded with what remained of these horses. Today the Appaloosa is the second largest breed in America. With its 'you-name-it-and-I'll-do-it' temperament and striking coat patterns it's not surprising. (You can actually feel the spots when they've got their winter coats.) The skin of the Appaloosa is pink and its hooves, which are exceptionally strong, are usually striped. The names of the different patterns of spots echo their Indian inheritance – names like Spotted Blanket, Leopard, Snow Flake, Raindrop, and Frost.

Each year more and more people come together with their Appaloosas to commemorate Chief Joseph's amazing journey and to ride a hundred miles of the trail through the mountains.

Now a few Appaloosas have arrived in Britain, where their speed, stamina and temperament are already much admired.

But beware, there are a lot of spotted ponies and draught horses around which are not Appaloosas. Spotted horses were drawn by early man in his caves in France, but whether those horses were true Appaloosas must remain a mystery.

The Appaloosa of today should stand 14.2 to 15.2 h.h. and have the markings and quality of the famous Nez Percé 'Palousy'.

Behind the Scenes

Horses always look wonderful on film, and filming them can be fun – that is, if the sun doesn't disappear, the rain stays away, everyone remembers what they are supposed to do and say and, of course, the horses understand why it all has to be done 'just one more time'. But however hard and tiring it may be, it's always interesting.

The original idea for a film story can come from almost anywhere. It may be something that someone in the production team thinks of suddenly, hears of or reads about. There are lots of ideas, but not all are good and most have snags. But if everyone likes an idea, Kina Murray, the unit research assistant, will then set about finding out everything about the subject and the people involved. She will propose a possible treatment for the item, suggesting when it might be done and how.

When this is known, Diana Sedgwick, the producer's assistant, will book a film crew and make all the necessary travel and hotel arrangements.

As soon as possible, the director or producer goes to the location to meet the people who will actually be in the film, see the horses and work out how he will film the story. He takes with him

In the office – I discuss a forthcoming project with Kina Murray, the programme's researcher, while Diana Sedgwick, the producer's assistant, makes our travel arrangements.

On location – David Turnbull and I deciding how to film a sequence.

The film crew in action ; the camera ready to roll.

Kina's treatment suggestion to discuss it with the people on the spot and if it's possible I will go too.

The way in which the story will be 'shot' must be worked out exactly : How much can be managed in a morning or a day ? Are lights required ? When will the horses be required ? When can filming start and by what time must it finish ? What can be cut out if there isn't enough time ? Where will the sun be, if there is any ? Where are the best camera positions ? Is any special equipment or lens required ?

At this stage the story is broken down into sections, called 'sequences', and shots, and a 'shooting' script takes shape in the director's mind as he makes his notes.

When the director returns to the office the project is discussed with the producer, David Turnbull ; a shooting script is then written, a detailed schedule of each day's work is worked out, and a list of all the equipment required is sent to the film operations manager.

FILMING

The first thing you have to come to terms with when you are filming is that nothing happens exactly as you hoped it would. People suddenly become tongue-tied, horses become nervous or over-friendly, and the farmer next door decides to plough up his field on the other side of the fence, and you can't hear a word anyone says !

Time is what you need most, so we often have to arrive on location at the crack of dawn. After a welcome cup of coffee (thank heavens for Thermos flasks !) the day's work begins.

The crew usually consists of a cameraman and his assistant, and a sound recordist and his assistant. Sometimes you need an electrician if lights are required, and sometimes you may even need two crews. Also on the scene are the director and the producer's assistant, whose official job is to make detailed notes of everything that is shot, but in fact she ends up doing a million other things as well. Each shot is identified by the clapperboard which has a shot number and a 'take' number on it ; several takes may be required before the cameraman, the sound recordist and the director are satisfied.

The second thing you have to get used to is that it is very unlikely that the story will be shot in the order in which it will be shown. To save time and moving the camera about unnecessarily, or perhaps to make it easier for the horses or the people involved, it is usual to arrange the shooting so that all the shots needed in one place or involving a certain person are done together. When this happens the director and the producer's assistant have to be very careful that nothing is missed out and that there are no errors of continuity (e.g. appearing in one shot with a horse looking over my left shoulder, and in the next with it peering over my right).

RUSHES AND EDITING

As soon as filming has finished the film negative is sent off to laboratories to be processed over night, and if you are lucky you can see a 'rush' print the next day. The 'rushes' are viewed every morning by the film operations manager to make sure that there are no technical problems with the film, caused, for example, by a fault in the camera. Obviously you must know about this right away in case you have to re-shoot. It may not be possible to do this, which can be heartbreaking and a problem for the director who will now have to work out how to get round it.

Viewing the rushes also gives the director a chance to see what he has shot and how it will go together. Some shots will be really exciting and pleasing, others frustratingly disappointing.

Having seen the rushes the director has to work out an assembly order for the film editor, George Auckland. George has edited the programme since it began and has made a real contribution to its success. The film editor starts putting the shots together as the director has suggested. But it is not as simple as that. Shots have to

Back at Television Centre watching the rushes with John Campbell, the film operations manager, and his assistant.

be 'cut' together so that the story flows along in an interesting way, and is told in a certain time.

FINAL EDITING AND DUBBING

The 'rough cut' will probably be twice as long as the finished film and won't flow perfectly, but it will give the director a good idea as to whether the story works as a film or not. Together, the film editor and the director view and review the rough cut, taking out shots and even sequences to make the film work better and to get it to the right length. Sometimes really nice sections that you've worked hard to get just have to go. The editor

brings a fresh eye to the story and will often see things that the director doesn't.

At last we have a proper film – but without sound, and this is where the 'dub' comes in. The editor and his assistant, David Wilson, start selecting and laying all the sound tracks required for the film. It's surprising how many extra effects are required to enhance the actual recorded sound. A sequence can be transformed into something quite magical by adding the right music, and to help tell the story clearly, a commentary has to be written. Recording the commentary is a tricky and precise business.

When everything is ready, the film is projected in a dubbing theatre onto a screen with a footage counter underneath, and the commentary is recorded. Then all the sound effects and original recorded sound are mixed smoothly together and balanced, and any music added. Finally, the commentary, the music and the effects are all mixed and blended together. It's always an exciting and rewarding moment.

Now the film is ready for transmission.

In the cutting room with George Auckland, the film editor, discussing the final version of the film.

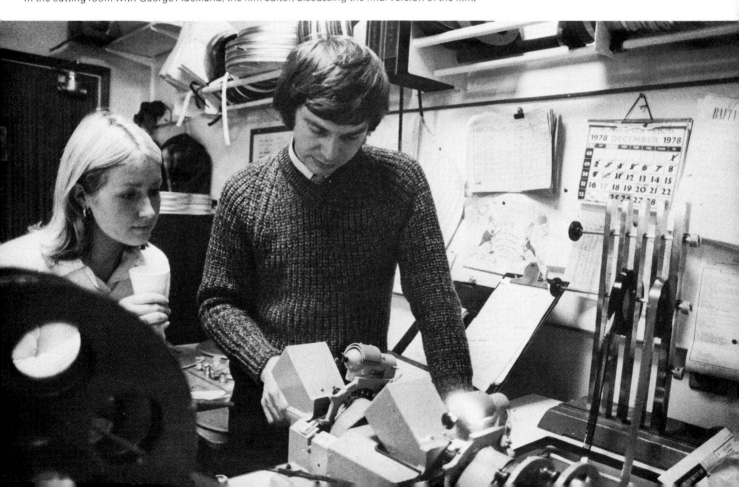

A DAY AT YOUNG'S BREWERY

Years ago there used to be thousands of heavy horses at work in towns throughout the country and there are still a great many more than you might think. One of their more popular uses is in some of our London breweries. I had the chance to visit the brewery belonging to John Young, the famous Young's Brewery of London which still uses Shire horses for local deliveries.

John Young believes in putting his animals to good use and finds that using Shires for short journeys is far more economical than lorries (the Shires are only used for deliveries within a three-mile radius).

When I arrived at the brewery I was surprised to find not only some of the most beautiful Shires in the country but also a complete farmyard. Roaming around the grounds, complete with a delightful pond, were ducks, geese, chickens, peacocks, sheep and even a nanny goat! I would never have believed that all this lay hidden behind the wall which separates the brewery from the main South Circular one-way system around Wandsworth! It's quite amazing and anyone can see it. Mr Young allows the public to take a look round his property since he likes the young and the old to see something of Nature, which is often very difficult if you live in the heart of London.

John Young prefers that his horses are put to work than allowed to lie idle in fields for the rest of their lives, where they would become bored and stale.

He keeps about eight to twelve working pairs of horses for delivering beer to pubs, and another eight or nine as a show-team.

The man in charge of these horses, the stable-manager, is Mr Harry Ransom. He is also in control of running the stable-yard. It's a very responsible job, but Harry has some very good men working for him. One of these is Michael Flynn, who is the main coachman in the show-ring.

Each Shire is cared for individually and gets the best food possible. They are fed extremely well in order to keep up the hard work. Plenty of bran and chaff, with a little whole hay or grass. As a special treat each horse also has a quart of ale mixed with its mash every day!

I was lucky enough to go out on one of the rounds with a pair of Shires driven by Michael whose correct title would be 'drayman'. The drayman always has an assistant, known as a 'tounser'. In the old days the tounser stayed on top of the dray cart and pushed the barrels down to the drayman, who took them down to the cellar. Nowadays, of course, it's a case of off-loading crates instead of the old-fashioned barrels!

One of the biggest Shires at Young's, in fact probably the biggest in the country, is Henry Cooper, who stands at 18.2 h.h. He is absolutely enormous, as you can see from the photograph. I could hardly sit comfortably on him he was so large. I made sure I stayed well away from his feet!

Shoeing is vitally important for horses which have to cover up to

Above: A farmyard? In Wandsworth?   *Below:* Loaded up and ready to roll.

Sitting on top of the world – Henry Cooper, 18.2 h.h.

sixteen miles in just one day. At Young's they have their own blacksmith's forge and a farrier comes regularly to hot-shoe the horses. Shoes put on in this way seem to fit the foot better than those put on cold. You can imagine the size of the shoes. They are really heavy, and at least four times as big as an ordinary little pony shoe.

The working harness is not very pretty. Its use is practical so it is made simply, for strength and durability, which matter a lot when you think of the weight these horses are pulling every day. But when I was shown round the tack room where all the show harness is kept, my eyes nearly popped out of my head! It was absolutely beautiful. Cleaned

regularly and ready for any occasion, it shone like silver. And the beautiful patent-leather harness was so shiny too. Just imagine the amount of time spent cleaning collars like these – possibly the largest in the country!

The main rule when cleaning harness of any sort, and that includes tack for your own pony, is to take every piece separately. Clean every buckle and every strap no matter how small it is. All the leatherwork should be washed with saddle soap, sponged down with clean water then rubbed dry with a clean cloth. If it's been neglected for any length of time, rub in some neatsfoot oil to keep it supple.

The show harness belonging to Young's is decorated with lots of horse brasses, and when out on parade the whole turnout just glitters. The horse too must look his best. Firstly, he must be clean. So if the weather is not too cold, he gets a complete wash-down, feet as well. (You can buy special horse shampoo, but I have to say that at home we use ordinary washing-up liquid if there's no shampoo!) After washing, the horse must be kept warm and put in a stable with lots of clean straw.

When he is completely dry he can be prepared for the show. Heavy horses always have their own forms of decoration. Their manes are usually plaited with braid or coloured ribbons, and their tails the same. Chalk powder is put on their white legs, and their hooves are oiled. After a final rub with a soft cloth our Shire is ready.

Young's are noted for their magnificent team of eight Shires. Driven by Michael, four pairs of horses are hitched together and put in to a brewer's dray.

They really do look fantastic – and unbelievably well-behaved. (Although I dread to think what would happen if they did decide to play up!)

During the year at Young's each horse has about a month's holiday. Rather like us, horses

The collar behind me is the biggest in the country.

need a rest once in a while. So John Young sends his Shires to a farm well away from the smoggy London air. The horses have the time of their lives, rolling in the mud and getting as dirty as they possibly can. Their shoes are removed, which allows the feet to 'breathe'. This does them the world of good, particularly after being on straw or peat for months. After the holiday they are brought back to the brewery and once more start their job of delivering.

The Shire is a particularly good type of heavy horse for this work as he has strength, stamina, adaptability, patience and docility. The only thing he lacks is speed.

When the Shires finally get too old to work they are turned out to grass, to spend the rest of their days in peace. (There are, in fact, one or two places in this country which are retirement homes for these horses.)

Apart from working in the city, heavy horses are becoming more and more popular with farmers all over the country. They can definitely do some things that a tractor might find difficult. One thing a farmer can be sure of is that he will always be able to start his horse in the morning! Horses are far better than tractors at coping with steep hillsides and are also far more economical. Not only that, but they can be used for breeding and showing – that's something a tractor can't do!

All over the country, ploughing matches are held throughout the year and anyone can go along to watch. I recently went to the All England Championship Ploughing Match at Windsor. It's

amazing to see so many horses working in one large area, all using old-fashioned ploughs and all quite at home, moving up and down the rows so gracefully. There is also a National Shire Horse Show held annually at Peterborough, if you want to see them.

Happily the heavy horse now has a secure future in this country, thanks to the many heavy horse enthusiasts and dedicated people who are still willing to work alongside this great animal.

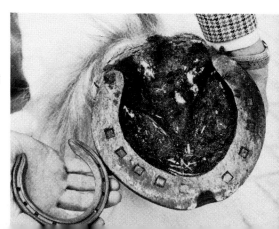

A blacksmith's-eye view of Henry Cooper's foot. The shoe on the left belongs to a 14.2 horse.

HORSES AND ME

As I've said before, I owe my whole career, as it stands so far, to our Welsh Mountain pony, Cusop Blighter, but horses have been very important throughout my whole life.

From a very early age my father had a strong interest in horses. He bought his first horse soon after he came out of the army at the end of the war. From thereon things progressed and it wasn't long before he had quite a few horses, his favourite being a skewbald filly called Lady. In fact, we still have her, and she is now a grand twenty-seven years old and still looking extremely well.

At that time my father used to drive Lady in harness to a milk-float and entered her in various trade classes in shows throughout the country, although he was never very successful. He noticed that the smaller ponies seemed to win almost all the private driving classes (this is where the whole turnout is judged, i.e. the driver's capabilities in handling the horse, and the vehicle itself). It was then that my father decided to buy a little pony for himself. And that's when Cusop came along. My father had a friend in Wales who bred Welsh Mountain ponies and sold us this little grey pony.

Before this I had had almost no interest in horses whatsoever, although my parents tried everything to persuade me. When I was quite young they bought me my first little pony, a piebald Shetland called Sparkle. She was lovely, extremely kind and a very good first pony. I used to enter fancy-dress classes on her, dressed up as a black-and-white minstrel along with a friend. We did extremely well and won a great many prizes, but I was still not terribly keen on riding (as you can see from the photograph).

Next, my father bought me a little palomino Shetland stallion called Kim, also a little governess car and a set of harness. But still I just didn't want to know.

Later on, when I was about eleven years old, I started going to my local riding school and my favourite pony there was a little piebald cross-Shetland called Whisky. I continued to go to the riding school for several years and this is where I received most of my basic riding instruction.

At the age of thirteen I had my first proper riding pony. His name was Cobweb, but alas, he was just that little bit too much for me to handle. It seemed that horses and me just didn't get on!

But when Cusop arrived things

At three and a half years old, riding was not one of my greatest pleasures.

Left: My mother and I are presented to The Queen – a proud moment for us both.

Even fancy dress couldn't make me smile.

did start to happen. Every weekend was taken up with going to horse shows. My mother would spend an hour in the morning plaiting Cusop's mane while my father would be preparing the trap and harness and loading up the horse-box; I would make us all breakfast. This routine went on right up until last year, when we thought that Cusop should retire whilst he was still winning, at seventeen years of age.

My life at home has always been very busy, and still is. Apart from the dozen or so horses that we keep, we also have some sheep, ducks, goats (for milking) and two dogs. It's not a particularly big smallholding but nevertheless it keeps the whole family occupied. Every weekend the stables have to be mucked out, apart from in the late autumn when we turn the animals out so they can have a short rest in the fields. We are kept pretty busy, too, with the goats. Arabella is mine and is the first goat we ever bought. She is a Saanen, and a beautiful white colour. We are supposed to take it in turns to milk her but we generally end up battling out whose turn it is, and the argument is usually resolved by me doing it!

In the spring the lambs are born, and it's a really lovely time. Every morning we rush out to see if any more have been born during the night. Sheep usually 'drop' their lambs at around six o'clock at night or six o'clock in the morning. I think I've only once seen a lamb being born during all these years.

In the summer, of course, it's haymaking time. We have only one field to make hay from, and once again the whole family is roped in to help. My mother drives the lorry (or tries to) around the field, my father stacks whilst my brother and I throw the bales up. It's pretty tiring work. I dread to think what it would be like if we had hundreds of acres to cut.

And so it goes on, but this year my father hopes to bring out a couple of new ponies to drive. We will still take Cusop to some of the bigger shows though. He really does seem to sense when he's going out and definitely looks forward to it.

One of the most important shows we attend is the British Driving Society's meet at Smith's Lawn in Windsor Great Park. Every year they have a meet with many different driving classes for all the people belonging to the society. 1978 was an extremely good year. It's not very often that my mum sits up with either my father or myself on the trap, but this year she did, and it was super because we were one of seven chosen out of a hundred or so competitors, to be presented to The Queen. A couple of years back, I had accompanied my father in being presented but we never thought for one moment that we would be chosen again. It was terrific!

Overall, I have been extremely lucky, particularly with the fact that I have a much-envied job and one which has helped me a lot with my riding.

Twice I've been asked to take part in jumping competitions at Olympia, although neither have been very successful! We've also made a programme on a jumping and event course in Ireland, which I tried my hand at. It was quite good fun actually, although I think I had one of the best horses to take me round.

Apart from actually making programmes about horses, I'm often asked to go along to small local shows and gymkhanas to present prizes, and this year one of the most amazing things happened. I was asked to go along to a show being held in aid of Riding for the Disabled and one particular little pony looked very familiar. It turned out to be Sparkle, who is now nineteen years old and teaching disabled children to ride. It was quite a moving moment for me and I'm really glad to know that she is doing such a marvellous job!

Cusop Blighter in action.

Off to the Races

No matter where you are in Britain, you are never very far from a racecourse or a flat-race meeting. Have any of you ever stopped to think of the amount of hard work that is involved in producing a horse for a race meeting? Well, before we started filming this particular programme, I know that I certainly hadn't.

By the time a horse is ready to run, the trainer, stable lads, head lad, farrier, vet and jockey will have put in months of patient work to ensure the horse's success and fitness to run.

But the most important person responsible for the horse is, of course, the trainer and one of the top racehorse trainers in this country is Brian Swift. Brian lives in Epsom and trains about forty horses a year, all of them worth thousands of pounds. Brian has a good horsy background – his father was a big bookmaker years back, and Brian has been a jockey himself, so he knows a lot about horses and racing.

I asked him what he thought helped to make a good and successful stables like his own. His first answer was obviously to have good horses. Also necessary are a lot of hard work, good reliable staff and, in his view, just a little bit of luck.

Brian works extremely hard, seven days a week, and has just one holiday a year during the winter months, when the racing and training season slacken off. Once the season starts, he has to be around the whole time.

Not knowing anything about racehorses, I wondered if Brian actually bred his own stock. More often than not, he buys them in, sometimes working through a blood-stock agency. When looking for new horses he usually goes to yearling sales, which are held all over the country. As a trainer Brian knows exactly what to look for in what hopefully will be a good, fast horse. An intelligent head and a bold eye are good signs, along with a good strong stride. A horse

Brian Swift.

74

Above: Walter Carter, the head lad.

Below: Under the watchful eye of Brian Swift, stable lads set off for an early morning ride.

which walks well will probably gallop well.

The yearlings Brian buys are given a couple of days to settle in to their new homes; soon after, the procedure of breaking them in begins. It must be remembered that at this stage the yearlings have never had a saddle on their backs and have to become slowly accustomed to it, like any other horse. It also may seem rather young to break a horse in, but just think, some of these horses are actually racing at two years old!

Each horse is an individual and to keep such valuable horses fit and happy means giving them the best possible care and attention every moment of the day. That day starts early, at 5 a.m.

The first person to visit the horses in the morning is the head lad, Walter Carter. His first task is to prepare all the feeds which are then given out by the stable lads when they arrive. Walter's job is an extremely important one in that he is the link between the trainer and the apprentices, the staff and, of course, the horses. The head lad is directly responsible to the trainer for the smooth and efficient running of the yard. He will know all the horses as individuals, in fact, just as well as he knows his staff and apprentices. Walter is as vital to the system as the horses are themselves!

After the lads and lasses have arrived first thing in the morning (and by 'first thing' I mean as early as 5.30 a.m.) the work begins. Each lad or lass has maybe two or three horses to look after, and within half an hour they will have their horses mucked out, groomed and tacked up ready for morning exercise. There are usually two rides and Brian will often ride out on both in order to study each horse's fitness and condition. If he doesn't go out, he is always around to check the horses and to give advice to the riders.

Each horse's daily exercise is well worked out and also very varied. Brian is very lucky because the Epsom Downs are just near by and this makes his training more convenient. He can use different parts of the Downs on different days. One track on which they ride is an all-weather track. It was developed to solve the problem of exercising the horses without damaging their legs when the ground was either too hard and frozen in the winter, or too hard and dry in the summer.

After the ride, the horses are

walked the last mile home in order to relax them, both mentally and physically. They are also allowed a swift nibble of grass just outside the stables. At this point, Brian may mention anything he may have noticed about any horse to its lad. For instance, the morning I was there one of the lads was asked to hose down his horse's legs because Brian thought the horse looked a little stiff. Both Brian and Walter have developed a keen eye for the horses' well-being; something which is essential in a yard such as this.

Once the horses are back in their stables, Brian will go around and have a good look at them. Attention to detail is so important and a part of every trainer's day. The lads and lasses will have cleaned the horses down by now, and the stables will have been cleaned out. Brian encourages his staff to wash round the horses' faces, not only to clean them but to help the horse wake up! By ten o'clock the yard is spotless, and many of the lads will have gone for their coffee break, meanwhile Brian continues the work on the day's schedule.

As soon as the young horses have become used to their new home, the job of breaking-in begins. Walter and one or two of the stronger and more experienced lads have the task of putting on a roller. This accustoms the horse to having something tied around his stomach. Some horses take to it easily, others not so. It needs a strong hand to hold them as they try to shake off that strange thing round them.

It is most important that you don't give the horse too much

Every morning the horses are given a routine face wash with a damp sponge.

Mucking out is a daily chore too.

exercise too soon. Bit by bit, is the golden rule. After a couple of days he will be quite used to being lunged with the roller.

Also the horse has to get used to the bit. This, too, is a slow process and much patience is needed. As soon as he has been 'mouthed', long-reining can start and it won't be long before he is ready to be backed.

This is the time when a brave person is needed. Gradually, he climbs further and further on to the horse's back, while someone holds the horse, of course! After a couple of weeks, and plenty of training, the horse is ready to be ridden.

As soon as the young horses are well handled and broken-in they can be introduced to mock starting stalls. It's important that the horse is given confidence right from the word go, so at first he will simply be walked through,

and given a bit of grass as a reward. He must be shown that there is nothing to be frightened of.

This particular lesson is an important one to learn as some horses suffer from claustrophobia and become extremely nervous of the starting stalls. If this happens when they get to run in a real race and are put in the starting stalls, they can cause a great deal of trouble to other horses and to the official starters.

Great care must be taken of the legs and feet of any horse, more so in the case of a racehorse. Brian and Walter check their horses' legs every day for signs of heat or strain.

'No foot, no horse' is a very old saying and nowhere is it truer than in a racing stable. At least twice a day, before and after exercise and last thing at night, the horses have their feet picked out and carefully oiled to keep them in perfect condition. No-one is more concerned with the horses' feet than the farrier, and in Brian's stables, he sees them every day.

Thoroughbred horses have very small feet in relation to their overall body size and weight, but however small, they are still vital.

The racehorse wears two main types of shoe: shoes for every-day use and a special, light-weight shoe, known as a 'plate', for racing in.

A horse will have plates fitted every time he races, which might be once a week. The blacksmith takes the plates off after every race and replaces them with the working shoes. He tries to use the least possible number of nails and, if possible, shoes into the same nail-holes each time, so as not to make too many holes in the horn and create weakness. In this way the plates will last for about four or five races. The normal working shoe lasts approximately one month.

The horn around the hoof grows continuously and needs to be cut back and trimmed approximately every four to six weeks. The hoof will take nine to fifteen months to grow from top to bottom.

It's essential to prevent the shoes from wearing thin. If a shoe should cause an accident or a plate become loose during a race, the result could be disastrous, both for the horses and for Brian.

Another vital factor in a racing stable is the horses' foodstuff. Large quantities of oats are given out daily, along with bran (which provides roughage) and some lucerne, which is a type of dried grass, similar to clover, and very

Slowly and gently the horse is introduced to the roller.

Starting stalls can present problems, but the horse must be shown that there is nothing to fear.

rich in protein. Some of the horses are also fed racehorse cubes. Giving each horse the right amount of food is critical. It's interesting to know that some horses may lose as much as two stone just by running a race.

Finally, after months of hard work, Brian will decide whether a horse is ready to run or not. We were lucky and managed to accompany Brian to a race meeting in Brighton.

On the day of the race, it is the responsibility of the travelling lad to take care of the horse due to run. It is also his job to ensure that everything is loaded into the horse-box. Spare bridles, head-collars, rugs, bandages, grooming kits, buckets, haynets, sweat rugs, medical chest – in fact, absolutely everything that may be required for any sort of emergency. He must also remember to take the owner's colours or racing silks which will be worn by the jockey at the race meeting.

When the horse arrives, it is taken to maximum-security stables which are out of bounds to everyone except the people directly concerned with the horse, namely the jockey, trainer and travelling lad, all of whom have to wear special identity passes. This is obviously to prevent people from trying to dope the horses or interfering in any way. The horses themselves do not come out of these stables until just before the start of their race.

The jockeys, too, are kept well under supervision and are weighed, along with their saddles and bridles, just before the race.

Before the 'off' the horses are walked round the paddock, then the jockeys mount and everyone canters up to the starting point.

At the starting point I spoke to one of the officials and asked him what his job actually involved. Officials travel round the country to the sixty or so official racecourses which have meetings three or four days a week. The stalls, too, travel round to different meetings. They are fairly expensive and not many courses have their own. Each stall is numbered and the positioning of each horse is decided by a draw.

The stalls are electronically operated and the starter is situated at the top of the rostrum with a long lead and button. As soon as he gets the signal that all the horses are safely in the stalls, he presses the button, the gates open and the horses are away. It was then I realised why Brian puts so much effort into training for the starting stalls. Any horse which causes difficulty, or which refuses persistently to go in, is 'black-listed' and must pass a stalls test before he is allowed to race again.

By this time everyone was getting very tense, including our film crew who had all put money on Brian's horse, myself included!

Well, they were off, and I found myself leaping around cheering furiously for Shocking Miss. Imagine my delight when she came in first! It was fantastic and I was clapping like mad, but Brian took it all quite calmly. We celebrated the win over a glass of champagne (thank heavens I'd finished doing all my pieces to camera!).

As a trainer, Brian finds he gets far more pleasure out of his horses than he ever would riding

Rolling in sand relaxes the horses after work and helps groom them.

them, even though he used to have a lot of fun as a jockey. If anyone is interested in becoming a jockey, can I just say it is not particularly glamorous. It's a very hard life, especially when you get to the top. Jockeys have to work a six-day week and often an eighteen-hour day, sometimes attending two meetings at opposite ends of the country in the same day. It certainly is a hard slog to the top.

Brian often has people writing to him to ask if they can become apprentices. You do have to be fairly small and light to start with, and if he thinks you are suitable, he will take you on for a trial period of about six weeks during the summer holidays. Some are lucky and recieve an apprenticeship, but from then on it's hard work all the way, no matter whether you are a boy or a girl. Everyone is treated in

exactly the same way, and it may be quite some time before you actually get to ride in your first race.

So the next time you visit a race meeting, or watch one on the television, you will realise being a jockey, an owner or a trainer is not all glamour. To be successful requires team effort, a great deal of hard work, and even more essential, a very talented trainer at the helm !

Brighton Races, before the 'off'.

The Csikós of Hungary

The famous Hungarian Post – definitely not for novice horsemen, or the faint of heart!

Hungary is a land of horses and horsemen. The Hungarians, or Magyars as they are properly called, were originally a nomadic people who came to Europe on horseback. About a thousand years ago they rode down from the steppes of Central Asia, and moved west onto the plains of Europe. Their long journey ended by the banks of the Danube, where they settled. Unlike other nomads, the Magyars kept their horses and soon they were the most renowned horse breeders in Europe.

It was especially thrilling to go to Kecskemet, right in the middle of the Great Plain of Hungary. The Great Plain covers half of Hungary and is still roamed by huge herds of horses. This is the land of the Csikós, the famous mounted herdsmen of Hungary.

Most of the Csikós still spend the whole of their year working with the horses on the Plain, living in semi-permanent camps. Their families, however, now live in or around the stud farms which have grown up all over the Plain.

The Great Plain comprises three principal areas : the largest is the Hortobagy ; the two smaller areas are called the Mezöhegyes Puszta and the Bugac Puszta. ('*Puzsta*' means wasteland or desert and though the land is very sandy, 'plain' seems a better word.) You can tell which area a herdsman belongs to by his clothes and saddle. On the Hortobagy they wear dark blue shirts with black waistcoats and trousers. Their hats are black and flattish with upturned brims. On the Mezöhegyes and Bugac Pusztas they wear white shirts and trousers with tall cone-shaped hats. But on the Mezöhegyes they wear black waistcoats and on the Bugac red waistcoats. Their boots are made of lovely soft leather but they don't tuck their loose baggy trousers into their boots ; instead they cut them off level with the top of the boots. (I don't know why this is, I imagine it must be very uncomfortable.)

The most fascinating difference between the herdsmen of the three areas is in their saddles. On the Hortobagy they ride with a very light felt and leather saddle which has stirrups but no girth. It's called a *patrache* and when you first see it you wouldn't believe they could use it. But they do. They fling it on with one hand, hold it firmly with the other, pressing down on the top of the off-side stirrup leather as they mount. On the Mezöhegyes the herdsmen use ordinary saddles, but on the Bugac they ride without saddles at all. Why ? Well, if the herds move off suddenly, the Csikós can mount and be off after them without delay. In fact,

The Csikós train all their horses to squat like this. In winter, riders will shelter against the horse's forelegs.

they seem to do everything at great speed. Interestingly though, they never trot – tradition, and perhaps the saddles, don't allow it.

The winters can be bitterly cold and to keep out the icy winds the Csikós put on huge thick sheepskin waistcoats. But whatever the season they always carry their individually decorated stock whips. Each whip has a short, thick wooden handle and a long (perhaps as much as twelve feet), thick thong which makes a very dramatic crack. The Csikós practise cracking their whips for hours, for this is how they turn and drive the herds – and they need to be

good, too, for a herd of horses is no easy thing to control. The herds' foals are weaned very late running with their dams while the herdsmen work, so they quickly develop tremendous trust in their men. I saw one foal lying with its head in its herdsman's lap while the man just talked quietly to it. The Csikós train each horse to lie down, and to sit like a dog, so that the herdsman can rest against the horse's forelegs or shelter there from wind and rain.

The Great Plain of Hungary – marvellous, intelligent horses and remarkable men who truly do have 'horses in their blood'.

Combined Driving

A Polish competitor on the cross-country phase of the World Driving Championships, 1978.

This is the sport that HRH Prince Philip made popular, and popular it certainly is. Though men have been driving horses in harness for centuries, it was Prince Philip's enthusiasm for driving that led to the first British National Driving Championship being held at the Royal Windsor Horse Show in 1970. A year later the first European Championships were held and in 1972 the first World Driving Championships took place in Münster. It was won by the British team who held it for two championships before losing it in Holland.

In comparison to other equestrian sports, driving is very much the new baby. The competition, which is often split-up and run over three days, is divided into three sections : Presentation and Dressage, then a tough cross-country drive known as the Marathon, and finally Obstacle Driving ; the Marathon offering the most points and being the highlight of the event.

There are classes for teams of four, pairs, tandems and singles, divided again into classes for horses or ponies. The most spectacular classes are the teams of horses or ponies which, of course, require more skill and horsemanship to manage, though tandem driving (one horse or pony in front of another) is also very skilful and exciting.

The competition is run on a penalty basis, i.e. you lose points rather than gain them. In Presentation the judge is looking at the over-all impression created by the turn-out. This includes the driver and grooms. Everything must be correct and spotlessly turned out, including the horse or horses.

The Dressage test is not spectacular to watch and is certainly difficult to understand unless you know what to look for. It's rather like the compulsory figures section in a skating competition. The test lasts for ten minutes and consists of a series of set manoeuvres and changes of pace. It's a test of the driver's skill and the horse's obedience. It's pretty difficult to do with a single horse or pony so you can imagine the skill required to get pairs and teams to respond and work as one.

The Marathon covers between 17 and 25 kilometres of roads and tracks, through woods and park–land, rivers and rough country. The course is divided into five sections. Sections A, C and E have to be carried out at a trot, and sections B and D at a compulsory walk – not so easy. Timing is crucial throughout as competitors

One of the Hungarian teams negotiating the Obstacle Driving course. Kecskemet, 1978.

are penalised for not completing a section between the time allowed and the minimum time. For example, Section A, to be carried out at trot, might be 8 km long with a time allowed of 32 minutes and a minimum time of 30 minutes. So the driver has to pace himself and maintain a speed of around 15 km/h – without the benefit of a speedometer, of course.

In Section C, which is also the fastest section, drivers have to negotiate several natural or artificial hazards or obstacles, such as extremely sharp turns,

banks, gates, log-piles, or rivers. You can, of course, use the same vehicle throughout the competition if you wish, but because many of the vehicles are old and very valuable most competitors use a specially strengthened vehicle and comfortable harness for the Marathon as this is where the thrills and spills come.

Obstacle Driving is really a speed competition, but it demands great skill and accuracy. There are usually seventeen obstacles, yellow cones with rubber balls on top,

set out in a twisting course, rather like a show-jumping course. Pairs of cones are set apart just 50 cms wider than the vehicle, so you have to be careful if you don't want to knock a ball off.

Today there must be a driving event somewhere in Britain every weekend with people driving everything from a simple pony-and-trap to a grand team of four. If you do take up driving there's a horseman's superstition : the collar is always put on first – or an accident will ensue. (You have been warned.)

Bridleways

Do you know how many bridleways there are in your area, and that it's important to use them?

WHAT IS A BRIDLEWAY?

A bridleway is a path on which you have the right to ride or lead a horse. You need no one's permission and your right to use the way cannot be taken away.

HOW DO YOU FIND THEM?

An Act of Parliament in 1949 obliged all County Councils to prepare maps of all bridlepaths, footpaths and roads used as public paths in their county. You can get copies of these maps from Her Majesty's Stationery Office and from certain other bookshops. What you want will be the Second Series of Ordnance Survey Maps (known as the six-inches-to-the-mile or 1:10560) for your area. If a bridleway is marked on the map, it is legally established forever. A further Act in 1968 requires Local Authorities to erect signposts for bridleways and where necessary put waymarks on them. This Act also made it unlawful to plough over rights of way on headlands.

IF IT'S NOT ON A MAP

If a bridleway you know is not marked, or if you think a marked footpath may really be a bridleway, you will need to make a search.
The following reference sources may help:

Old maps of the area can be found in local libraries and museums, and these may show that you have indeed found an old bridleway. You may have to use your imagination when looking at these old maps though. For example, if a map shows a way running between two hedges it suggests that the public had rights over the way and the farmer had to fence his livestock off. Or a map may show a way leading directly to an old forge or mill to which the public obviously would have had access; or it could be simply the shortest route between two villages.

Railway maps which show the proposed routes for early railways are excellent as are the *Turnpike road maps* published in 1837 and *Canal maps*.

All the maps mentioned above can be seen in your County Archives Office or at the House of of Lords Record Office, London, SW1, on giving twenty-four hours' notice.

Extracting information from maps:

1. Always use a pencil to avoid marking maps with ink or biro.
2. Remember to note the name and date of the map.
3. When you have made your notes get the librarian to sign and date them as correct.
4. Never take a tracing without permission.

An official copy of a map, if you want one, will cost about £2 and your order will take about six weeks to fulfil.

Another source worth trying is the local residents. Old people may remember a way being used as a bridleway. It is particularly important to find out how it has been used in the last twenty years.

IF YOU BELIEVE IT IS A BRIDLEWAY

Write to: The Secretary of the Bridleways Organisation, The British Horse Society, The National Equestrian Centre, Stoneleigh, Warwickshire CV8 2LR

This organisation will certainly help. Your local riding club, riding school or branch of the Pony Club should also be interested and helpful.

FOOTPATHS ON PRIVATE LAND

You can ride on a footpath if it crosses private land, and the owner has given you permission to do so.

KEEP BRIDLEWAYS OPEN

It is important to use your local bridleways, otherwise they will become overgrown, blocked, forgotten and lost, maybe for ever. If your bridleways are getting overgrown, tell your area Highway Authority or the landowner and offer to clear the bridleway yourself. If they agree:
1. Remember, this will be hungry and thirsty work.

2. Be sure of the exact route of the way and its width.
3. Don't burn the rubbish without permission.
4. Write a letter thanking the landowner afterwards.

YOUR RESPONSIBILITY

Although you have the right to use the bridleway at all times be considerate and sensible and you will be welcomed by landowners and farmers.

ALWAYS

1. KEEP TO THE ACTUAL BRIDLEWAY (especially when crossing private land.)

2. SHUT ALL GATES.

3. RIDE SLOWLY PAST LIVESTOCK. (Try not to ride through herds of milking cows or flocks of sheep at lambing time.)

4. RESPECT CROPS. (Take special care in wet weather.)

5. SHOW CONSIDERATION TO WALKERS AND CYCLISTS (they may be splashed or scared ; give plenty of room, specially to children ; look out for picnickers ; also watch out for dogs – ask their owners to call them up if necessary).

DON'T
RIDE WHEN THE BRIDLEWAY IS WATER-LOGGED OR CUT-UP.
DO
TRY TO GET TO KNOW LANDOWNERS AND FARMERS. BE A WELCOME GUEST NOT A NUISANCE.

OBEY THE COUNTRY CODE.

Country Code

The Country Code is a series of ten reminders based on common sense – and common failings. So when in the country remember:

Guard against all risk of fire.

Fasten all gates.

Keep dogs under proper control.

Keep to the paths across farm land.

Avoid damaging fences, hedges and walls.

Leave no litter.

Safeguard water supplies.

Protect wild life, wild plants and trees.

Go carefully on country roads.

Respect the life of the countryside.

Making a Hay-net

Rather than pay a lot of money for something which you could easily make, why not try this method of making a hay-net?

You need thirty-three lengths of string saved from bales of hay or straw.

Take three lengths of this string and plait them together. Then tie the ends so that the plait forms a ring.

Onto this ring tie the remaining thirty pieces of string using ordinary slip knots. Make sure they are securely fastened with as little wastage as possible.

Then, taking two strings at a time, about 4 inches down, tie a knot by simply making a loop and putting the string through itself. (Easily done but not so easy to explain, so take a good look at the picture!)

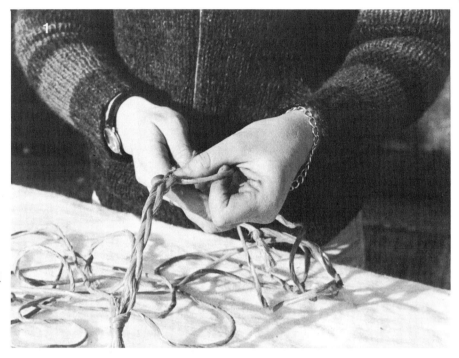

1. Plait together three lengths of string.

2. Make the plait into a large loop by tying the ends.

3. Onto the loop tie thirty strings of equal length, using a slip knot to secure them.

4. Give each string a tug to make sure the knot is good and firm.

5. Take two adjacent strings and tie them together with a simple knot about 4 inches down their length. Work all the strings in this way.

6. Next, pair and tie the strings so that a lattice-work pattern is formed. Continue working until you reach the end of the strings.

Do this all the way round with each pair Then repeat the process about 4 inches down but pairing the strings so that they begin to form a sort of lattice-work pattern. Carry on doing this all the way round until you can no longer tie the strings together.

To finish off, tie knots in each pair of strings as near to the ends as possible, then thread a small piece of string through all the knotted strings, gather and tie off.

If all has gone well, you should have a complete hay-net. It certainly is a money-saver, and if your horse is one of those who likes to chew through his hay-net, at least you can make another!

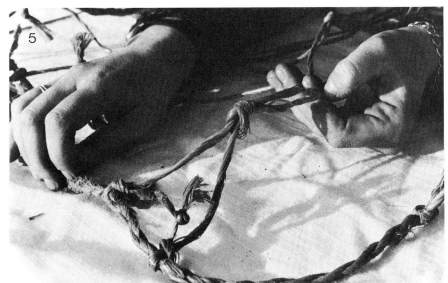

7. Finally, knot the end of each pair of strings and pass a small piece of string through the knotted strings. Gather and tie off. You should now have a perfect hay-net.

Show-jumping with Paddy McMahon

If you want to produce a programme about show-jumping, you can have no better adviser than Paddy McMahon, one of Britain's leading exponents of the art.

Paddy lives in Oxfordshire with his family, his dogs and, of course, his horses. From a very early age Paddy showed obvious talent for riding and jumping, and it wasn't long before he was competing at events all over the country. He soon rose to international fame and his outstanding successes with Fred Hartill's amazing horse, Pennwood Forge Mill, are well remembered.

In 1973 Paddy turned professional and is now producing some of the best show-jumping horses in the country. One such horse is Red Sea Serpent, which you can see Paddy riding in our pictures. I'm sure we'll see a lot more of this great combination in the near future.

So last summer the 'Horses Galore' team went to visit Paddy at his home, taking with us our own 'guinea-pigs', so that he could advise them on their riding and jumping, which would also help anyone watching at home.

Kate, Sharon and Biddy were up very early that morning preparing their horses for the journey. They were also busy preparing themselves, as it was quite nerve-racking for them!

They were all at different stages in their riding, Biddy being more of a beginner than the others. She had a chestnut pony who, I'm sorry to say, was just a little bit lazy. Poor Biddy had to keep on at him all the time to get him going.

Kate had a little palomino pony, very fiery and very good at jumping, which is a great confidence builder when you are first learning to jump.

Our last show-jumper was Sharon who was already quite experienced, her trainer being Brian Crago.

When we arrived at Paddy's the sun was shining and it was a lovely day (which makes a change – usually when we go out filming it decides to rain!). Just down the lane was a large field, perfect for us to film in. Right from the word 'action' we all

Paddy McMahon and Red Sea Serpent.

started to learn many new things about jumping.

A show-jumper must be an all-round equestrian, possessing sound knowledge, skill, patience and most certainly a good sense of humour! As Biddy, Kate and Sharon each took their turn in showing Paddy their capabilities, we began to see how many problems there are.

Jumping is totally different from ordinary riding. The rider's seat, or position in the saddle, is a very forward one. The stirrups are about three or four inches shorter than the length you ride with on the flat so as to enable most of the weight to be absorbed at the knee and into the stirrups. Once you become an accomplished jumper you use whatever length of stirrup suits you best.

When you first begin it's no use trying to jump large fences straight off, even if you think you have the skill or the nerve. It must be a gradual build-up, starting off with ordinary poles laid out on the ground and progressing to cavaletti work. This is good for both horse and rider; it improves a horse's balance, rhythm and co-ordination and helps to keep him alert. After these preliminary stages you can work up to a small jump, making sure it's not too difficult for the horse. It's quick and easy to write this down, but it takes months for you and your horse to achieve perfect harmony, particularly if you are both novices.

One of the most important things to learn is how to develop an independent seat. By this, I mean allowing the horse to jump more easily and thus be less hampered by the rider's weight.

Easier said than done! Also remember that the rider must maintain contact with the horse's mouth the whole time, making sure that the hands remain relaxed and supple and following the movement of the horse's head. In this way you interfere less with the horse's action.

Paddy explained that you must sit deep in the middle of the saddle and move everything from there, and without letting your legs flap about. When you move forward over the fence, your knees should stop on the saddle with your heels pressed down. Paddy says he relies completely on his legs and never carries a stick.

Confidence is the keynote. Both horse and rider must have it and the early lessons are very important. You should encourage your horse to enjoy jumping and allow him to develop confidence in his own ability, all the while establishing a good seat and style.

Whilst we looked on, Paddy showed us what he meant by a good seat and how to jump with style. When someone like Paddy shows you how to do it, he makes it look so easy, you begin to wonder what you were worried about. (In fact the only person who looked worried was our cameraman who was positioned directly alongside the jump – however, his fears were totally unnecessary.)

If your horse is young and 'green' (this means new and inexperienced) it's important that he must not be 'overfaced' – that is to say, he should not be urged to jump obstacles which are too big for him too early in his career. Poles placed along the ground

help to make the horse use his muscles and also loosen his back, encouraging the lowering of his head, which improves suppleness. It does take a long time.

Once you've overcome the difficulties of these small fences, start popping him over anything you come across (within reason, of course!); things like small logs, ditches or banks, so that the horse gradually begins to accept jumping as part of his work.

Your aim, remember, is to have complete control over a supple and obedient horse. Control of the hindquarters is most important as this is where the horse's power and propulsion come from. Hill work is good for building up these particular muscles, and for getting the back legs really working and strong.

In the approach to an obstacle, a horse which jumps well will lower his head and stretch his neck in order to assess in advance the size of the obstacle and the point in his stride at which to take off, which is also controlled by the rider. The head and the neck are the horse's main balancing points. In fact if you watch a horse jumping, you'll see the extension of neck and head right out in front before his forelegs leave the ground.

As your pony stretches his neck to jump, never bridge your reins over his neck. If your hands go up his neck, you're not allowing him to stretch forward properly, so let the reins and your hands go down to his mouth.

In the moment of suspension over the jump, it is most important that the rider looks forward in the direction of travel. This was one of the points Paddy kept repeating to our riders, who constantly found themselves looking down toward the ground.

There are five phases to a jump: approach; take-off; moment of suspension; landing; and getaway stride. The rider has four things to consider: determining the horse's track; regulating impulsion and speed; riding accurate turns; and finally, avoiding possible refusals.

For the approach the horse must be in a collected canter and facing the jump so as to be able to judge the height and spread, while the rider determines the speed of approach. During the horse's strides prior to take-off, the rider's legs must be firm but ready to move to encourage more energy, should he sense any possibility of a refusal from the horse. The rein should be light and the contact constant, but 'elastic' enough to 'give' as the horse leans forward.

If your pony rushes his fences, stop him in front of a fence, let him stand, and give him a titbit to distract him from the fence. Do this a few times and he'll soon quieten down.

Once you've landed, always look forward to the next jump, keeping your impulsion going, as this is when the horse is likely to slacken up a little. He's also likely to lose impulsion coming out of a corner and many faults occur as a result of badly ridden corners. Remember, most show-jumping courses will have at least two changes of rein, so it's important to learn to ride your corners well.

If, when you change rein, your pony changes legs on the front but becomes disunited at the back, you can put this right with lots of groundwork. Paddy advises riding a figure-of-eight which gets smaller and smaller, to balance him up behind and make him change on all four legs.

Finally, if your pony is going forward in the bridle he can't do much wrong, so keep him going forward all the time.

There is obviously far more to this subject than I have managed to tell you here, and only lots of practice will really help you to improve.

Paddy stipulates that children must enjoy their riding. It's not fair to make people and children do things they do not want to. Never expect an inexperienced rider to bring on a novice horse

Sharon, Kate and Biddy, our guinea-pigs, get some tips from Paddy.

Sharon putting theory into practice.

or pony – a young rider should be taught his trade by riding ponies that know how to jump well. From my own experience at my local riding school when I was much younger, I would thoroughly recommend basic and early training by a proper instructor. I realise that lessons are very expensive, but if you think it is going to cost too much, offer to lend a hand mucking-out or grooming in return for a free lesson. It's well worth it!

The Pony Club, one of the largest youth organisations in this country, is a world-wide organisation and affiliated to the British Horse Society. It is particularly interested in training young people to be all-round riders. It's certainly worth joining; you don't have to own a pony and it's lots of fun. Different branches organise instructional rallies in riding and stable-management and try to help people to know more about their ponies and the responsibilities and care that are necessary.

When you are sufficiently competent, then it is possible that you may be asked to represent your branch in inter-branch competitions in one-day events and show-jumping.

The most important thing of all is to enjoy yourself, to have fun and make the most of your pony. If show-jumping doesn't appeal to you – and I have to say that I'm not keen – then try something else. For me, riding around on the nearby common is just fine.

Paddy shows us how it should be done.

HORSES GALORE HORSES GALORE
GALORE HORSES GALORE HORSES
HORSES GALORE HORSES GALORE
GALORE HORSES GALORE HORSES
HORSES GALORE HORSES GALORE
GALORE HORSES GALORE HORSES
HORSES GALORE HORSES GALORE
GALORE HORSES GALORE HORSES
HORSES GALORE HORSES GALORE
GALORE HORSES GALORE HORSES
HORSES GALORE HORSES GALORE
GALORE HORSES GALORE HORSES
HORSES GALORE HORSES GALORE
GALORE HORSES GALORE HORSES
HORSES GALORE HORSES GALORE
GALORE HORSES GALORE HORSES
HORSES GALORE HORSES GALORE
GALORE HORSES GALORE HORSES